Standing On The Brink — An Education For The 21st Century

An Anthology of Essays on Waldorf Education

Edited by

Stanford Maher

and

Ralph Shepherd

NOVALIS PRESS

CAPE TOWN

NOVALIS EDUCATION SERIES

STANDING ON THE BRINK —
AN EDUCATION FOR THE 21ST CENTURY

Essays On Waldorf Education
Edited by Stanford Maher and Ralph Shepherd

Educating for Creative Thinking: The Waldorf Approach by Joan Almon, reprinted from *ReVision*, Volume 15 No. 2, with permission from the Helen Dwight Reid Educational Foundation. Published by Heldref Publications, 1319 Eighteenth Street, N.W., Washington, D.C., 20036-1802.

The Movement That Everyone Tries To Forget by John Davy, reprinted from *The Times*, London, 23rd March, 1973.

Published by Novalis Press, P.O. Box 53090, Kenilworth 7745, Republic of South Africa.

Typeset in 9.5pt Times Roman by Prototype Graphics and Documents, Cape Town.

Printed and bound in the Republic of South Africa by Mills Litho (Pty) Ltd, Cape Town.

First published 1995.

ISBN 0-9583885-1-2

CONTENTS

Foreword

It is sometimes argued (I know the argument) that civilisation has always been on the brink. It does not matter what the historical time is, human society appears to be at the edge of the precipice.

In a sense, though only in a sense, this is right. Education is precisely related to the brink, or precipice, or chasm, which always beckons societally. It is the thing (we call it an institution) that creates — can create — vision for us, every time, to make us pull back from the brink; or even, amazingly, if we have gone down, to make us resurrect.

All the great healers of history were teachers.

If humankind's story is a matter of brinkmanship, the truth is that the chasm of our time is utterly terminal to life. At the end of the twentieth century, in the words of Fritjof Capra, "we find ourselves in a state of profound, world-wide crisis. It is a complex, multi-dimensional crisis whose facets touch every aspect of our lives . . . a crisis of intellectual, moral, and spiritual dimensions: a crisis of a scale and urgency unprecedented in recorded human history. For the first time we have to face the very real threat of extinction . . . of all life on this planet".

Joseph Camillerri — some years before Capra — considered that our "contemporary human crisis is so profound and pervasive that the very attempt to analyse it — let alone resolve it — seems to defy the power of human reason and imagination".

Where do we go from here?

I suggest this answer. We should be seeking vision as never before. We should be searching for teachings of real — of great and greatest — human worth. We should be seeking for the feet of great teachers, to sit by them. Education of substance is the answer.

This, I believe, is the point of this book, and the point of "Waldorf Education".

But what can we mean by education of substance? I understand these essays to be responses to this question, philosophically, and practically as far as "the classroom" is concerned. The thoroughgoing consciousness of philosophical bases in and during the actual event of teaching and learning, at whatever level, is a hallmark of the good teacher; which means also that good teaching is teaching that cultures pupils themselves to consciousness of philosophical bases from the very beginning of the teacher-pupil relationship.

The entire atmosphere of this kind of relationship — whatever the activity or the lesson — is one of a questioning consciousness of values. The social work educator Ruth Wilkes once wrote that "the absence of moral philosophy as part of the core curriculum (of social work) was a fatal flaw and led to the uncritical acceptance of value as instrumental to the social worker's purpose without any reference to the notion of value itself". I believe that the substance of this view can, for its pedagogical correctness, be generalised to all enterprise that bears the name of education, and to the phenomenon of "curriculum" in general.

In short, education of substance is education that is built around this centre of "the notion of value" and which, in relation to it, is conscious of and honestly declares its value-choices — needless to say in a spirit of critique and self-critique. It is "open" education: education under the auspices of freedom.

Concerning the shadow-side of what is called education, it is astounding how more often than not in "educational circles" at every level — in our primary and secondary schools, in our universities no less, and with our "educational planners" — there is an obliviousness to the philosophical presuppositions of what is taught and learned. "Education" turns out to be an intellectually blind wading through "knowledge". This is the real ground of "rote learning", amazingly held — held fast, and often arrogantly — by teachers, or rather would-be teachers, who are the very ones to denounce rote learning most loudly!

Waldorf education as "education for a civilisation on the brink", is — to witness this timely collection of essays — education that lives outside the shadows: value-conscious education. This volume is timely in the sense that should its kind of thinking be taken seriously wherever it occurs in our world, no doubt humankind can pull back from the brink. For South Africans, it is timely also in this sense: we find ourselves here and now at the historical moment of a gargantuan task, trying our hand at educational transformation and restructuring in the aftermath of the havoc in schooling wrought by apartheid. Within this context I believe that should the vision of this book be taken seriously by our educational planners, there is firm ground for our hope of a truly new South Africa.

Prof. Adam Small
February 1995.

Introduction

The following essays on education are written by educators most of whom have stood in front of people of different ages and have experienced that awful responsibility and that inner delight of being a teacher. The ideas they write about are not just theoretical ideas. And, since each of us is at some time or another a teacher, whether formally or informally, these educational and practical issues affect us all. This is especially true as we face the future in this country, where new impulses will need to inform each person, so as to ensure the freedom we have just begun to experience.

Parents I speak to are impatient of an educational system that does not develop and renew the life forces in their children. Their children are bored. The teachers I work with and speak to, express a deep sense of frustration at being forced to work with material they have to present to disinterested children year in and year out in a prescriptive manner.

Someone once wrote that it takes about 15 years for a really good educational idea to reach the level of the classroom! When we add to this, the heavy ideological traffic off–loaded by politicians meddling in educational matters, it is little wonder that very little innovation enters the classroom door. When it does, it is usually through the individual efforts of brave and persistent teachers. Despite all the massive shifts that have occurred in this country recently and around the world, so very little has really changed in the world of education. It seems as if the authorities are trying to solve educational problems using the same methods that created the problem in the first place.

At present there is a lot of talk going on about education. Among different interested groups around the world, much is being said while the search goes on for an educational approach, which will assist developed and emergent societies in addressing their many social, economic and political problems. Parents and educators wait eagerly while these conversations proceed at conferences and workshops. Long and erudite papers are published and noises are heard near and afar — but nothing changes.

Is it perhaps because the language hasn't changed?

I believe we are going to have to teach ourselves a new educational language. I don't know exactly what it sounds like or what it's called yet. The articles appearing in this volume sound real and contribute significantly to the formation of this new language. They sound harmonious and balanced, with a human touch.

Parents and teachers need to be informed of this new language about education, because it affects everybody. This new educational language speaks to the heart, without denying the intellect or neglecting the heart-felt desire for active participation. The language is invitational and open, full of enthusiasm and drive. My hope is that, as these articles are read, we may start to learn this new educational language. And, as it is learned and used it will grow and help bring about a renewal of education in this land.

Dr Martin Fisher
February 1995.

The Novalis Institute would like to thank the Embassy of the Japanese Government in South Africa for their assistance in meeting the costs of publishing the Novalis Education Series.

Their generous contribution towards this project is an expression of the support of the Japanese government for teacher education in South Africa.

1

THE DUAL CRISIS IN SOUTH AFRICAN EDUCATION

Elizabeth Dostal

Modern education systems in almost all countries of the world are based on the same model:

- of teacher/pupil interaction in a classroom situation;
- of transmitting knowledge about various disciplines in a compartmentalised fashion according to nationally prescribed and accredited curricula which nevertheless follow the international trends and;
- of being pronounced and controlled as a public good by the state.

This universal education system is grounded in a particular world view which is mechanistic and reductionistic. It believes that by taking a system apart and understanding its parts and compounding this partial knowledge, the whole is known. It also holds the belief that if one knows enough one can manipulate and control the forces of nature. This mechanistic thinking gave rise to the advances in science, technology, and mass production which characterised the industrial age — an age lasting from before the 1800s up to about World War 2.

This universal education system as we know it today evolved during the industrial age together with all the other cultural, techno-economic and political institutions as we have come to know them. Thus, during the industrial age, the education system co-evolved in a harmonious manner with all other aspects of life in societies engaged in industrialisation. It therefore served these societies well during this particular stage of their development. However, this education system is now and has been for some time in crisis in both the First and Third World for different reasons, namely:

- Large sections of societies in the Third World are still in a pre-industrial stage of societal development either with a subsistence agricultural lifestyle in rural areas or an urban lifestyle on the fringes of pockets of urban industrialised life;

- Rapid technological advances in the First World pushes these countries from the industrial age into an information age.

In both cases, the current societal reality does not match the lifestyles, ways of thinking and assumptions on which the industrial age education system is based. Education is out of harmony with either the rapid progress of especially the techno-economic sphere experienced in the First World, or with the lack of progress in the Third World. Some societies, like South Africa, embody both a First and Third World sector. Thus both types of education crises are operative.

The Education Crisis in the Third World

The education crisis in the Third World is characterised — amongst others — by the following two major issues, namely:

- Inadequate education facilities compounded by rapid population growth, poor economies and education policies that favour the ruling classes — South African apartheid education being an especially obnoxious example of this;
- Problems regarding the school readiness of large sections of Third World populations, due to cultural differences and cultural transitions.

While the issues concerning education facilities are well known, the cognitive and knowledge-related issues concerning school readiness are often ignored. Let us look at these issues in turn:

Provision Of Education Facilities

Third World societies all over the world are characterised by rapid population growth, giving rise to a world population unprecedented in the history of the world. The pupil and student explosions experienced in the Third World are one of the consequences of this population growth.

In South Africa in 1960 there were 2,6 million pupils of all races in school and by 1994 it had risen to 11,4 million. By the year 2000 pupils will number 14 million or more. This growth in pupil numbers occurs in the Black population, while pupil numbers in the White population have declined slightly over the same period, whilst the Coloured and Asian populations have been more or less stable since the late 1970s.

The rapid increase in the number of pupils requires an according increase in facilities and resources. In South Africa it implies — amongst others — the need to build 350 new schools per annum for 500 pupils each. The demand for the provision of equipment as well as teachers is growing accordingly. Most of the increase in education expenditure is absorbed by coping with this increase in numbers, leaving little room for improving the quality of education.

The combination of stable pupil numbers on the one hand and the higher per capita expenditure on White and even Asian and Coloured children during apartheid education, has led to the discrepancies in the quality of educational facilities between various population groups.

It is clear that the resources which provided an education for a small White population cannot meet the needs of the many. The same dichotomy exists between the rich and poor countries of the world: low birth rates are shared by Japan, Europe, the United States and the rest of the First World; wherever populations grew very quickly, the educational challenges are correspondingly greater.

No-one can minimise the cynical neglect of children's needs that has taken place throughout the school system in South Africa. Most schools for Black children have been under-resourced, with poor facilities, and in some cases, none at all. A visit to a single "school" in an informal squatter community will show the desperate nature of the circumstances in which thousands of children attempt to find their way into the modern world. In these "worst case" situations the picture is so bleak, so utterly neglectful, it would be easy to assume that Black education in South Africa is among the most poorly financed in any country. It is therefore surprising to discover that public expenditure on Black education in South Africa has been far greater than in many other Third World countries — and it has to be recognised that South Africa is a Third World nation, its First World trappings notwithstanding.

In the world's most developed countries, annual per capita expenditure on education is around US$700, dropping to about US$20 in less developed countries. Africa as a continent spends so little it hardly gets on the graph. In South Africa, average expenditure for all racial groups has been about US$100 per person. The figure for Black pupils alone — the most neglected community — is double that of less developed countries elsewhere in the world, and about four times the average for the rest of Africa. Expenditure on White education in South Africa has been about half of the average in the First World. At the time of writing, education swallows about 27 percent of Gross National Product. With health care facilities in dire straits, huge housing backlogs and unemployment at record levels, it is difficult to envisage the allocation of a greater share of the national cake to education.

School Readiness

The problem of material resources is what is generally spoken of in our mechanistic, measurement-oriented age as "the crisis in education". It is assumed that by making inputs in teacher training and providing enough textbooks and classrooms, we will be able to offer the majority the kind of education which has been enjoyed by the few. However this kind of material provision — basic and necessary though it is — barely scratches the surface of the problem, for education is less about facilities than it is about Mind. I have touched on this by introducing the problem of the educational model inherited from western nations.

The First World educational model has proved inadequate for the Third World because it is out of harmony with the institutions of pre-industrial societies. Its content and methodology is completely unsuited to the needs of people drawn from a pastoral lifestyle into an urban economy, without the preparation necessary to assimilate an education based on First World technology and concepts. This would be true even if sufficient early childhood education had been provided, but the almost total absence of pre-schools for Black children makes their entry into primary school that much more difficult. Too many children are failed in the early classes because they do not understand the basic concepts and have not developed the necessary cognitive skills which are demanded by modern education systems. The problem is compounded by language issues, especially in the urban areas where ethnic groups intermingle.

It is especially the recently urbanised populations which are affected by the cultural transition from an agricultural to a modern industrial/information society. In this respect, many Africans are experiencing now what happened to many Germans during the 1800s, and later to Afrikaners during the Depression years of the 1930s. Predominantly rural dwellers, Africans' home backgrounds have had little contact with the modern world. The knowledge gap is too big for them to deal with because the dramatic cultural shifts which have occurred, in common with many Third World countries, lead very quickly to a breakdown of meaning.

Cause-and-effect thinking applies in the First World. In the shift from rural life to urban industrial living the cause-effect relationships are broken down. The people caught up in these migrations then find themselves unable to understand how the world works. Their children, arriving at primary school for their first taste of formal learning (there are almost no pre-schools for Black children) cannot acquire the necessary basic development from their home backgrounds. The result is that they are unable to develop the foundations for thinking. In particular, they cannot cope with a school situation in which the curriculum has been developed for First World requirements. The high failure rate in the lower school classes in Black communities is a direct outcome of this. By the fourth year of primary school half of all children have been excluded from the system. The pattern then extends into the secondary school, where many students have a grasp of the learning content which frequently is shallow in the extreme and is limited to theoretical concepts.

The Education Crisis in the First World

This brings us to the second crucial aspect of the education crisis, one that few people appear to be aware of — that while the mass of South African society is only now preparing to enter the industrial age, the leading nations of the First World are leaving that age behind. It is this factor, added to the situation outlined above, that constitutes South Africa's dual crisis in education.

The First World is moving into an information age. The process started after World War 2, but is only now in the electronic era gathering momentum. It is accompanied by growing evidence that developed nations are finding their streamlined, high-tech educational systems inadequate to the task.

One of the mind shifts involved is that we are realising that the Universe is more complex than we thought and that we cannot control it. Also, there are complex social and ecological issues we have not come to terms with — political and economic restructuring and linkages between industrial development and ecology. How do we cope with the enormous unemployment in the Third World, new kinds of diseases, urbanisation, knotty social problems and endemic conflicts? There is talk of Africa being marginalised because it is seen as a continent of declining economies, continuing political conflict and civil war. But it is not only Africa that is in trouble. The collapse of the communist empire in Europe, as well as the ongoing civil war in the former Yugoslavia, aptly demonstrate the current difficulties regardless of whether socialist or capitalist oriented governments are "in charge".

Everywhere we look we find that things are complex, non-typical, radically changing and inter-related. We are disturbed to realise that the comforting stability of the industrial age is gone, and that the institutions and value systems which evolved during that age are collapsing. Technology has overtaken us and everywhere political, economic and social systems are in flux. While we thought the world was a machine, we could operate it — and the machines were simple. Also, we had not exceeded the ability of nature to absorb our negative output of waste and pollution. So the assumption that a little more technology could fix it seemed reasonable.

During the past few decades, reality has changed radically. In the First World the output of waste exceeds the capacity of nature to absorb it. In the Third World the growing population exceeds the carrying capacity of land. The result in both "worlds" is rapid environmental degradation which — if continued unchecked — may even jeopardise the survival of these populations.

We have started to recognise that by attempting to solve a complex problem, we seem to make it worse. A solution in one area creates new problems in many others. Moreover, information flows have made the world very small. There is now a world market and a world culture superimposed on individual cultures. There is also rapid change in every sphere. The products of education are bewildered in this new relativist, changing environment, with no solid foundations. The "facts" (and in some cases the abilities) they learned at school are not being asked for, because the questions have been rapidly replaced by new ones.

The volume of information, measured solely by the number of scientific publications, doubles approximately every seven years without taking account of proliferation through electronic and other media. The student's knowledge is out of date by the time he leaves school, so to stuff the children with information is pointless. In an effort to overcome this difficulty, the private sector in the First World has been spending a great deal of money on education and training to enable people to operate effectively. Now, however, the concept of training courses is giving way to that of lifelong learning.

What are urgently needed are *meta skills* which will enable pupils to find, apply and evaluate knowledge and to define and cope with complex problems. Not only does our education systems fail to provide these, especially in an educational setting where the teacher gives a pre-defined problem for the pupil to solve. Yet when the pupil emerges into the world she now finds there are no pre-defined problems, but that she has to identify the problem herself.

This concept of the context giving meaning is new to school-leavers, who find that out of school the problems don't come with a label attached nor with ready-made solutions. It is not only school leavers who are ill-equipped. As adults, we tend to react to problems out of our professional training, which has given us formulae, procedures and methods to work with. The truth is that a problem usually has many dimensions and spans many disciplines, but we are not trained to work with these or to co-operate with others in identifying and solving them.

While we thought the Universe was a clock all we had to do was study the clock. Now we are awakening to the fact that we are living in an evolving, purposeful universe and in a rapidly changing societal environment and that we need a new world view — one that realises the Universe is Intelligent! The Universe we are now becoming aware of is governed by *relationships,* out of which new creations are constantly arising. The properties of this universe are qualitatively different from those found in a machine world. It is a meta shift, equivalent to witnessing a clock maker who has worked with springs and cogs being introduced to a super-fast computer without having previously encountered electronics. Just as the operation of a computer cannot be understood by mechanical concepts, so it is proving impossible to operate in the information age using the thinking of the mechanical-industrial age.

What is it that is different? For a start, in *relationships* emergent properties arise. Something more is generated than the sum of the people involved. Symbiosis in nature affects places and people far afield from the source — the so-called "butterfly effect" spoken of in chaos theory. It is a concept with which we have not previously had to deal. "Ceteris paribus", meaning "providing everything stays the same" is a term used widely in scientific investigation: provided that everything in the environment stays the same we can predict certain things. We use this proviso all the time in research, but one of the things we are learning is that everything does not stay the same. These are some of the features of the information age and educational systems everywhere are out of step with this development. The result is that even industrial giants like Germany and Japan have found they share common problems in the field of education.

The general education system world-wide as well as in South Africa is grounded in this mechanistic, reductionistic world view in which the "ceteris paribus" assumption guides the organisation of knowledge. This world view leads to the belief that if we know enough we can manipulate and control our environment. We are beginning to discover that we cannot do that, so the premise on which our knowledge is founded is incorrect. It has taken some time for the nineteenth century rapture with the promise of science to evaporate, but the infatuation is proving to be just that. The embarrassment has been made all the greater by the admission by leading figures in almost every sphere of research that, as Fritjof Capra has stated in *The Turning Point*, we no longer have answers for the many urgent problems which are surfacing.

What are the Implications of this for Education?

The rational mind has difficulty when it finds itself in such situations, but aesthetic thinking can attempt to make sense of the patterns which manifest themselves. Our education systems have been geared to analysis because our world view is analytical, but we have reached the limits of analysis. In the complex environment we now live in, things arise out of interaction and we then have to synthesise in order to understand. Synthesis understands *patterns* — our ears detect the one instrument in an orchestra which is out of tune. But we have no world view that copes with synthesising . . . or have we?

This may be where Rudolf Steiner (Waldorf) education can make an important contribution. It is able to supply some of those aspects the information society needs but doesn't have. These include perceptual abilities and capacities which cannot be gained from an intellectual education, but only from an imaginative one. The difference in the capacities acquired is as stark as the difference between sticking a photocopied outline of a picture in a book as information to be recorded and memorised, and acquiring the ability to draw the picture oneself, using colour and form, which can provide a springboard for capacities in apparently unrelated subjects such as geometry. This first method is used almost universally in South African education, while few State primary schools seem to recognise the value of the second.

There are shifts in knowledge taking place now which are as fundamental as those which occurred during the European Renaissance. To renew education will require ideas and concepts which belong in an information age, and the process is happening so quickly that probably we have only one generation in which to discover and implement them. The essential thing is that education is about Mind, and there is an inherent irony here: it is in the information age that we are having to learn not to burden ourselves with information of the wrong kind! The flow of data is overwhelming for adults, let alone for children. Data alone will bury the pupil long before he has developed the capacities necessary to survive in this new world.

The Educational Policy Debate

As pointed out above, the shortage of educational and other facilities and the severe unemployment situation in South Africa, as in the Third World in general, are serious and are aggravated by the population explosion. But what is really holding back fundamental educational transformation is that the education debate is focusing mostly on facilities instead of on mind change. All this adds up to the current serious crisis in modern education. We need a more intelligent way of dealing with the problem, and this will mean changes in the content of education and in the way we deliver it. The most serious factor is that we are not recognising the situation and we are not doing very much about it.

There are many different approaches that help the transition from agriculture to a more developed culture, and many pilot projects that deal with various aspects of the problem. Examples are various bridging and cognitive development programmes, amongst others. There is also a body of knowledge available on how to move into the information age, namely systems thinking, alternative ways of dealing with conflict, cognitive and educational methods for developing holistic and lateral thinking, creativity, the aesthetic sense, imagination and intuition, amongst others. But there is no coherent strategy for renewing education in a creative way, which will nourish in children the qualities they will need as adults in the 21st century. Yet an innovative educational model exists, as for example Waldorf education developed by Rudolf Steiner. Rudolf Steiner has pioneered revolutionary concepts in the field of education and these have been tested in Waldorf education internationally for 75 years. Its understanding of child development, which is after all the foundation on which much effective teaching rests, is unparalleled but little known. It is based on a three-level approach to the learning process, to lesson planning and the rhythm of school life — namely the integration of the faculties of thinking, feeling and willing.

Because Steiner's Waldorf education is both art and science, and because it addresses the whole child, it is able to heal some of the illnesses in our present education system. In particular, it can help teachers and pupils in our primary schools who at present are struggling with abstract, dead information, as it provides a more enlivened and human teaching situation. Its emphasis on the development of the whole child could help to repair the damaged foundations of our system and redress the current situation, in which 50 percent of black pupils drop out by Standard Four. This is an appalling waste of human resources and at the same time a national tragedy.

The new methods have been put into practice and tested in enough First and Third World countries from Germany to Ecuador, to enable them to be evaluated. A practical question is: can they be introduced into mainstream State education on a basis which will prove effective for large numbers of pupils? In the main it is a matter of appropriate teacher education and training, but there is also a mind-shift involved.

Waldorf Education has also the potential to help us into the information age. Its philosophy, methods and techniques are fundamentally different from those used in conventional approaches to education. The irony, however, is that because it is so different it is regarded as somehow suspect, too unconventional and too complex. What modern education appears to be seeking is a philosophy and practice of education which will deliver all the results of a really transformative and modern set of methods — but one which will remain as familiar as the model we have been using for so long. It is unfortunate that although the new model has arrived so few have understood it, because it simply looks and feels too different.

2

WHY WALDORF? A COMPARISON WITH CONVENTIONAL SCHOOLING

Stanford Maher

This brief article attempts to depict in table form a comparison between the aims, values and methods of Waldorf education and those of conventional mainstream schooling. The use of the term "conventional" may appear dismissive, as meaning bland or ordinary. This is certainly not intended; the term is used merely to characterise many similar approaches to education, emanating from state departments and from independent schools, which have this in common: they set out to educate children largely through the intellect. This does not mean that they ignore the affective (emotional life) or the psychomotor (will) aspects of the child (though many do), but in the main, education is seen as the transmission of facts in the form of concepts to be learned through cognitive processes. The late Cecil Harwood, one of the founders of Steiner education in Britain, some 70 years ago, was a scholar who would never have stooped to denigrate the value of the intellect; nevertheless, he characterised the over–intellectual approach outlined above as one which "educates barely half the child." [1]

Steiner (Waldorf) education is unique in that it sets out to educate children holistically on three levels— through the intellect, the emotions and the will — in order to develop a balanced personality. There is still little formal appreciation outside the Waldorf school movement, of the seminal concept of the human being as a created threefold form, which Rudolf Steiner described as the necessary basis, not only for education, but for the structure of human society in general.

The other fundamental feature of Steiner education is its conscious, scientific approach to the spiritual–physical nature of the developing child and the ways in which the methodology takes account of this in each school year. Each year in a Steiner school provides not simply an increase in the difficulty of the content of the lessons, but an experience of a particular and unique stage in the spiritual and physical development of the child. As these concepts of threefoldness and the stages of child development are fundamental to understanding the differences between conventional and Steiner education, a brief description of each will be given.

The Threefold Nature of the Human Being

Steiner pointed to the concept of threefoldness as underlying all human experience of Creation, from the Trinity to observable phenomena in the physical world. He saw in the human form of head, trunk and limbs, the physical basis of the three human soul faculties of thinking, feeling and willing. It is the harmonious education of these three faculties which is the aim of Steiner education, and for this reason teachers work consciously with the threefold concept in all aspects of the education, from the goals of the pre-school, primary and high school sections, to the rhythm of the teaching day and the involvement of all three faculties in each lesson.

The head is the seat of conscious thought through the medium of the brain which is not merely a sophisticated computer, but operates more as a form of chemical mirror, in that it *reflects* the activity of the individual soul and spirit. The head dominates the nerve-sense system of the body and is quiet and still, an observer of the world.

The limbs and the digestive-metabolic system together form the polar opposite of the conscious thinking process. They are active without any directed thought and are the seat of the will forces. The trunk mediates between the other two regions and is in constant, untiring motion. The principle of rhythmic activity dominates the trunk through the pulsing of the heart and lungs and forms the basis for emotional life.

Steiner noted that in terms of *physical growth* the head is most formed at birth, the trunk and legs gradually catching up with it, while in terms of *consciousness*, the opposite applies: babies kick in the cot long before thinking is evident. The development of children between babyhood and puberty is therefore occurring on two levels, or in two opposing directions. Intellectual consciousness is therefore not a product of physical growth, though it is necessarily founded upon it, but a completely different force operating in the human being. Unconscious will activity governs the pre-school child, who gradually develops an ordered emotional life, and, much more slowly, the capacity for abstract logical thought.

Steiner advocated that educationists respect this process of the development of consciousness in children from activity, through the feelings to the thinking. This would mean that in the early classes from pre-school to second grade, the teaching should to a large extent be activity-based, the learning content having meaning for the young pupil because he learns by doing, as well as because of the appropriate emotional content it contains. Abstract information, on the other hand, has no meaning or reality for them. High school pupils are gradually able to operate out of thinking, a faculty they develop to an uncomfortably sharp degree, as many teachers and parents find to their cost!

Stages of Child Development: A Descent of the Spirit

Steiner teachers see children as immortal beings with spiritual identities, and hence a spiritual past and future. They do not educate children merely to achieve material success in a competitive, materialistic world. The child's life on earth is seen as a destiny through which development will take place, and lessons will be learned. This gives the context in which a meaningful education is to take place.

The spirit does not incarnate all at once into the new-born babe — if it did we would see many more Shakespeares composing in the crib. It is a gradual descent that is witnessed, through stages documented by many philosophers and psychologists, as the physical instrument is gradually enabled to express the being within. The preschool, primary and high school have very different tasks. On a more subtle and detailed level, the activities of the first grade will change in quality and meaning as well as in level of difficulty, with each successive year.

To enable children to carry out their life tasks as adults, their education must be geared to developing their innate capacities and talents, so that in the words of Rudolf Steiner, as adults "they may of themselves be able to impart direction and purpose to their lives." As spiritual individualities, children bring with them both specific talents and difficulties, and education involves the unfolding of the one and the healing, to whatever extent is possible, of the other. For this reason, the kind of person a teacher is may over the years mean more to parent, child and society than the professional qualifications he possesses. Seen from this perspective, examinations serve merely as an assessment tool on a rather limited level.

The education is tailored to children's needs in terms of the inner development processes they are undergoing, which are observable through physical, mental, emotional and behavioural changes. It is the teacher's task to understand these needs and to meet them in the most artistic and human way possible. As an example, fractions in arithmetic are taught in many schools as soon as a child shows the necessary intellectual ability to grasp them. However to have meaning for a child's development, they should, in the eyes of Steiner teachers, be taught after the age of nine years. This is the time when children pass from a subjective to a more objective understanding of their world, and when they are consciously taking it apart and putting it together again in their minds. The curriculum in Steiner schools, from Grade One to Matriculation, is tailored to the inner development processes which Rudolf Steiner describes. These do not conflict with conventional child psychology, but they do throw light on aspects which have up until now been left unexplored.

The Organisation of the School

Because the development of capacities is the aim, the teacher has the freedom to teach in the way he or she considers will achieve the goal. A firm curriculum exists for Steiner schools throughout the world, but teachers have the freedom to interpret and deliver it in their own ways, and to change the content and the pace to suit the individual children in their care. With an increasing number of children exhibiting learning difficulties, it becomes ever more important to match the pace and style of learning to individual needs.

Teachers in Steiner schools tend to stay with their class as long as possible during the primary school phase (6 to 13 years), in order to develop a deep understanding of each child. This enables problems to be approached from a viewpoint which would not be possible for a new teacher meeting the same class every year. There is close parent-teacher co-operation which includes open access to teachers and home visits by them.

The management and running of the school leaves educational policy decisions in the hands of the College of Teachers, which elects its own chairperson, while financial and legal matters are shared by parents and teachers co-operating on a school council.

---

1 Harwood, A C. : *The Recovery of Man in Childhood*, Hodder & Stoughton 1958. (Copyright: The Myrin Institute, New York, 1958).

Topic	Waldorf Education	Conventional Education
Educational Principles	The individuality of the child is equated with the concept of an immortal *spirit*, which relates to the body through the medium of the soul. All education of children involves bringing into harmony the physical body, which is the vessel, with the spirit which gradually reveals itself in the child, step by step, through observable processes of child development.	The issue of whether the child has a soul and spirit is not the concern of education, which concerns itself with Mind or intellect. The intellect is able to process facts and experience events and thus learn about the world. This is the core of education. Various approaches add to this the need to educate the higher sensibilities of the child.
Educational Methods	As the child has a threefold nature of thinking, feeling and willing, each of these should be fully involved in every lesson in order to integrate all three faculties of the soul. The teacher has the freedom to interpret the curriculum as she sees fit for the particular class of children which are her responsibility. She seeks to do this as imaginatively and effectively as she can.	Adult knowledge is distilled by experts in universities, colleges and educational departments, into forms considered necessary (a) for the overall needs of society (including industry and commerce), and (b) to pass the examinations which make possible the next steps in the educational process (senior primary, high school and university). The appropriateness of the content to the intellect of the growing child is considered largely on intellectual considerations. The teacher presents the material to the pupils at a rate set by the authorities (heads of department, principals, inspectors and higher officials). Those pupils who can cope with the rate and level of work are promoted, others failing. The only person who has full contact with the pupils — the teacher — has the least say in the process.

Topic	Waldorf Education	Conventional Education
Lesson Structure	Throughout primary and high school, the first two hours of each day form a Main Lesson in which a subject is explored as a block for three or four weeks. This allows for an in-depth approach and encourages concentration rather than fragmentation of the pupils' involvement. All of the seven lively arts (music, modelling, movement, speech, drama, drawing and painting) can be used to deepen the subject content and to learn it on different levels. This constitutes the Waldorf approach to integrated studies. It allows for wider and deeper exploration of subject matter (particularly in high school) than is catered for by syllabi geared to examinations.	Most lessons are of the same length (35 or 40 minutes) to fit the timetable, unless they are sport or specialist lessons. Many subjects are thus taught in rapid succession throughout the day. The accent in most lessons is on learning through cognitive processes. Each teacher expects the pupil's attention and their intellectual abilities to be at his disposal. There is limited relief for pupils from the constant pressure for intellectual performance and usually little artistic activity, since "arts" lessons are separated from conceptual learning.
Plan of the Day	Work which is intellectually demanding is performed early in the morning when pupils are fresh. Art, music and language lessons follow this and crafts are timetabled for late morning or afternoon periods. Each Main Lesson is structured to allow pupils to "warm–up" for the lesson, through speech, movement and music in the liberal arts tradition, and provides time for quiet intellectual work and for physical, practical or artistic activity.	Subjects are timetabled to suit the school system and teacher availability. Pupil needs may or may not be considered. Frequently, lessons are experienced in random order with little awareness of the child's changing receptivity during the day.

Introduction of Numbers in Grade One	These are introduced in story form as realities in themselves which have particular qualities. For example, *two* is the duality inherent in day/night; *four* is the structure for the seasons; and *six* forms the walls of a bee's home. The concept of number is associated with realities in the physical world which have qualititave differences.	Numbers are introduced as tools for calculation in arithmetic and to develop thinking abilities.
Introduction of Letters in Grade One	Introduced as shapes linked to the mental images contained in stories: a goose becomes a G, a house an H. Writing, a concrete activity, precedes reading, a more intellectually demanding exercise. Exercises in movement, modelling and drawing precede formal writing.	Letters are forms to be learned cognitively in order to acquire the ability to read and write. Reading is taught as quickly as possible in order to facilitate "real" learning.
Relationship between Curriculum and Pupil Age	The curriculum is designed to provide the experiences considered necessary to match the *inner* stage of development of the child. This means, for example, that fractions in arithmetic and the singing of rounds in music would not be taught while the child still perceives the world as a unity, but at the age of nine, when she begins to feel an observer of nature rather than a part of it — an indication that the spirit of the child is proceeding a step further into earthly incarnation.	The pupil's mental age is the determining factor. What pupils can assimilate intellectually is the guideline. Clever children are encouraged to learn as much as they can and may be placed above those suited to their emotional/ physiological stage of development.
Examinations	None during the primary school phase. All pupils are promoted on the basis of age unless there are serious learning disabilities which the particular teacher cannot cope with. Scholastic tests are conducted and pupils write the school-leaving matriculation examination.	Usually examinations are held throughout the school career. Promotion is determined by the percentage of knowledge acquired, as measured in examinations. In South African state primary schools children are now promoted without examinations. Teachers are required to assess their pupils, but as most of them do not do the activities which make such assessment real, it appears to have limited value.

Topic	Waldorf Education	Conventional Education
Gender Equality	All pupils are treated as equals with the same ambitions and needs. All learn to knit in the first school class. In the fifth grade girls begin woodwork alongside boys. In high school both do metalwork and woodwork.	Culturally determined depending on school and area. In many communities girls are prejudiced and seen as having fewer ambitions than boys. In high schools, girls and boys are separated, the focus on intellectual learning being regarded as more important than their learning about one another.
Moral Education	All subjects are permeated with respect for the created world and the dignity of the human being, amounting to reverence in the early classes. The aim is to enable the child to experience the Good, the Beautiful and the True in systematic progression, in pre-school, primary and high school respectively, as appropriate for their stage of development.	Respect for the values of society, and/or specific religious or other groupings is inculcated, depending on the type of school and the culture in which it exists.
The Structure of the School	There is no school principal or head teacher. All permanent teachers are equal members of a college of teachers which administers the school and sets all educational policy. Usually there is a school council on which parents and teachers are equally represented, and which takes responsibility for legal and financial matters.	Appointments are made by education departments. There is a top-down hierarchy in most state schools, with most teachers following defined career paths.
The Goal of Education	To assist each child to develop its inner capacities to the full in order to become a person of initiative, compassion and insight and to acquire the skills and knowledge necessary to work and contribute to society.	To give pupils the intellectual knowledge necessary to succeed in life, in accordance with their abilities; through sports, to develop character and competitive ability, yet be able to work as a member of a team.

3

EDUCATION FOR A CIVILISATION ON THE BRINK

A Basis for Renewal in South Africa?

Stanford Maher and Peter King

The greatest problem facing teachers and parents in South Africa today is the same as that facing their counterparts in Europe, Japan and the United States: we are not providing an education worthy of the human being. This may come as a surprise to some politicians, civil servants and planners, whose goals and concerns are generally quite different from those of most parents and teachers. The officials are (usually with good intentions) desperately trying to offer millions of pupils the best education the national budget and the available human resources will allow. They do this to acquaint them with the facts of life in the 20th century, to equip them to earn a living when they leave school and thereby contribute to the national economy. Along the way, it is sincerely hoped, the pupils will develop a sense of morality and generally acquire capacities for learning and living. To this mix, most politicians would add a healthy dose of patriotism and respect for the values of society — which in effect means those of the government of the day.

It is interesting that officials usually talk about pupils, often in relation to numbers and facilities, while parents and teachers talk about "their" children — a precious resource which they share in common. It is a telling difference. Most educators, politicians and civil servants, I believe, are humane and decent people who wish the best for the next generation and set out to equip them accordingly. However, sometimes narrow perceptions and vested interests play in and distort the process. The result is that an education system is produced which aims to meet the needs of government rather than of society as a whole or of young children in particular. This occurs when the school system is designed to turn pupils into politically compliant but economically energetic capitalists or communists, to suit whichever country one is looking at. In either case the result is the same: children are fitted into an educational system designed by a government with specific political, social and economic aims in mind. It is a goal doomed to failure because these aims refer to three spheres of society which operate out of very different natural laws. However, realities such as these are no obstacle to a determined planner and much misery is created for millions of vulnerable young human beings until the chickens come home to roost and the education system is seen for the hollow shell it is.

The crux of the problem is that since the European renaissance we have had a love affair with the intellect. This has led to the creation of a world-wide culture which worships intellectual learning and all its inventive offspring, and which discounts other aspects of the human being. Because the intellect is clever, amoral, logic and measurement-oriented and inherently superficial, it cannot but reproduce these features in whatever it creates.

Governments everywhere are under pressure because their countries are competing for survival in an increasingly sophisticated industrial world. Their solution is to turn out products from the education factories with the necessary technological edge — and so more maths and science are crammed into pupils as early as possible in their school lives, while artistic work such as painting, drawing and drama is minimised. Never mind the fact that the planet can only survive through co-operation, that it helps not a bit for America to outdo China, Taiwan, Singapore and Japan in business, the exercise fails anyway because it ignores the human element on which everything depends: the abilities of children are simply not designed to operate according to the demands of this system.

The influence of the underlying intellectual persona of our age cannot be overestimated; it is this which has led to children's capacities for learning being assessed largely from an intellectual viewpoint. Although lip-service is paid to the affective (emotional) and psychomotor (willing) parts of the young human being it remains only that, for these aspects are not fashionable areas for research. As such, they are neither understood nor properly valued. The result is that educational decisions are taken on the basis of inadequate information, and our children are placed under inappropriate and usually unnecessary amounts and types of stress. The huge increase in learning difficulties in schools is directly due to this excess stress factor, combined with increasing pressures in society in general.

If a bridge were built with such cavalier disregard for stresses and materials the engineers concerned would soon run out of job offers. Politicians and civil servants are able to sidestep criticism because the effect of the stress only shows up much later in life, when it is likely to be blamed on the parents and teachers anyhow. South African officials have in the past also been helped by a dispirited teaching profession which learned that those at the top could not be swayed from their course. At the time of writing far-reaching changes in education are planned which look impressive on paper and indeed appear to have many merits. However, seeing what is wrong with an existing system is always easier than designing and implementing one which will work better. All education systems are founded on views of the human being and it is the clarity, quality and accuracy of the vision which makes the difference. A view which sees young children as miniature adults, economic producers in embryo, will offer a very different education from one which sees them as complex and vulnerable beings struggling to find identity and meaning in a social and educational environment which becomes more difficult by the day. The vision is all-important because it determines the goal which will eventually be reached, for good or ill.

Among those who have assessed the modern love affair with the intellect as being at the core of our civilisation's problems have been Albert Einstein, Stephen Covey, Fritjof Capra, Rudolf Steiner and Vaclav Havel. Each has expressed it in his own way. Einstein pointed out that we have been trying to solve our problems at the same level of thinking on which we created them, indicating that a different kind of thinking is required. Both Covey and Capra speak about the need for new paradigms. Covey, speaking out of his long experience in the business world, says: "If you want to make minor changes, focus on behaviour and attitude. If you want to make quantum leaps, focus on the paradigm." As an example, he quotes the conventional tendency of many American companies to manage from the top down, seeking creative ideas only from within top management. A new paradigm would be the Japanese model in which leadership is seen as the ability to tap the creativity of an entire work force. Capra, in his seminal work, *The Turning Point,* says the Western world suffers from a crisis of perception:

> "We are trying to apply the concepts of an outdated world view — the mechanistic world of Cartesian-Newtonian science — to a reality that can no longer be understood in terms of these concepts. What we need is a new paradigm, a new vision of reality; a fundamental change is needed in our thoughts, perceptions and values."

Quoting the historian Arnold Toynbee, Capra points to uniformity and lack of inventiveness as symptoms of decline — evidence we can see as perhaps the fundamental characteristic of educational systems throughout the world. He also notes (as does Steiner even more forcefully) that the end of this century will mark the coming together of several important transitions which will create an unprecedented challenge to humanity.

Vaclav Havel, the playwright who at the time was also President of the Czech and Slovak Federal Republic, defined the problem in a watershed speech at an economics conference in Davos, Switzerland, on 4 February 1992. Analysing the reasons for the fall of communism in eastern Europe, he warned that this would be only the first of our modern ideologies to fall, only the tip of the iceberg of the dangers facing civilisation, being but "the perverse extreme" of what our current soulless thinking has created.

This is how Vaclav Havel saw the problem:

> "The end of communism is, first and foremost, a message to the human race. It is a message we have not yet fully deciphered and comprehended.

The end of communism has brought to an end the modern age as a whole. The modern era has been dominated by the belief that the world — and Being as such — is a wholly knowable system governed by a finite number of universal laws that man can grasp and rationally direct for his own benefit. It was an era in which there was a cult of depersonalised objectivity. Communism was the perverse extreme of this trend. The fall of communism can be regarded as a sign that modern thought — based on the premise that the world is objectively knowable — has come to a final crisis.

"We all know that our civilisation is in danger. The large paradox at the moment is that man is absolutely incapable of dealing with the danger. We cannot do it because we cannot step beyond our own shadow. We are trying to deal with what we have unleashed by employing the same means we used to unleash it in the first place. What is needed is something different, something larger. Man's attitude to the world must be radically changed. We have to abandon the arrogant belief that the world is merely a puzzle to be solved. The world, too, has something like a spirit or soul."

Vaclav Havel's words in many respects echo the thought of Dr Rudolf Steiner, the Austrian philosopher, scientist and educationist, some 80 years ago. Steiner expressed the same thought as Einstein — that people were trying to solve their problems with the kind of thinking that had created them in the first place — but he also hinted at the reasons for this. He said the social problems of the 20th century are mainly a result of facts confronting the human being *on a level to which he has not grown.* He said the human being lacks the necessary insight to solve such problems because *he always confines himself to the externalities of the facts he faces. This is why people are "socially helpless".*

The issues which Steiner warned would become critical for mankind, have still to be solved. At the end of the First World War Dr Rudolf Steiner, then lecturing widely in Europe, proposed a new threefold social order. He believed that the three spheres in modern society of political-legal rights, culture, and economics, though interdependent, operated out of different intrinsic laws and needed to be developed accordingly. Many modern thinkers believe that had his ideas been realised much of the conflict in the world which has arisen through the polarities of communism and capitalism could have been prevented. Although his vision of the underlying threefold structure of human society was not widely accepted, his creative genius has been widely recognised, and lives on in many other ways — in philosophy, medicine, art, architecture, religion and biodynamic farming.

Steiner believed that education naturally belonged within the sphere of culture and therefore needed to be free of State, religious and economic control. He initiated a new approach to education, which was first offered in 1919 to the children of workers at the Waldorf-Astoria cigarette factory in Stuttgart, at the request of its director, Emil Molt. It was probably the first ever "people's education". It offers insights and techniques which could heal and transform our rule-ridden, essentially joyless and shallow State education system. It is therefore important to examine the principles underlying it and the methods it employs.

"Waldorf," as it has come to be called, is a unique kind of education, fundamentally different from other methods, in that it approaches the teaching process both as a science and as an art. It is a complete *science of education* in that its approach to child development is based on knowledge of the whole child as body, soul and spirit. It is an *art of education* in that it requires the teacher to adopt an artistic approach to educating children in every subject, so that the soul can be touched by and the spirit understand the meaning inherent in what the intellect is processing. From the viewpoint of methodology, this means teaching on three levels to influence the child's thinking, feeling and willing through the learning content. It seeks to achieve what Vaclav Havel reminds us is so necessary if we are to survive the problems our technological age has created. It offers:

- A new way of looking at the world, seeing it as both material and spiritual, and thereby healing the conflict between science and religion.
- A new picture of the human being as a spiritual identity with a past, present and future, whose task is to use her individual gifts in community with others for the benefit of the earth.
- An education which because it is imaginative, can nourish the whole human being, including his moral nature, not simply the intellect which is responsible for so many of the problems identified by Vaclav Havel.
- An insightful curriculum which matches the learning process to the stages of inner growth in the child, and which therefore promotes appropriate, stress-free, enjoyable learning.
- An unparalleled grasp of child development which understands how education of the body and the intellect influences the soul and spirit.

Waldorf schools have been able to take root on every continent because of the essential humanness and practicality of the ideas. How the education is achieved is briefly explained in the notes which follow.

What is a Waldorf School?

Waldorf education is "free" education — that is it seeks to leave the child free in his inner self without requiring him to fit into a mould. The teacher's task goes far beyond the transmission of knowledge. Each child is seen as a spiritual individuality, clothed in a physical body, who encounters many difficulties in finding his way into life on earth. The teacher's primary task in the lower classes (pre-school and junior primary) is therefore to help the child to integrate and harmonise her soul faculties of thinking, feeling and willing, so that she may gradually unfold her innate capacities. As it is recognised that this task is a creative one, the teachers themselves are required continually to deepen their knowledge of the world and of humanity. They are not teachers simply because they have undergone a "training".

Waldorf schools in South Africa are part of an educational movement which now numbers some 1600 school initiatives around the world (see UNESCO *Brief*, Appendix 2, page 118). Because the schools in all countries are independent of state educational bureaucracies, their teachers have the freedom to develop their teaching creatively and imaginatively. The unique curriculum given by Rudolf Steiner and adapted to suit different cultures around the world, has been tested for 75 years. Its success can perhaps be gauged partly by the growing numbers of parents and teachers prepared to make many sacrifices and to forgo the state education provided for their children, preferring to place them in Waldorf schools outside the state system for the sake of their health and well-being.

There are also a number of teaching colleges which enjoy some form of official recognition in several countries, such as Britain, Sweden, Holland, Germany, Australia, South Africa and the United States. In some of these colleges, a training in Waldorf education is given which includes certification by the government. In others (in the U.S. states of New York and New Hampshire for example), colleges offer graduates officially recognised Masters degree courses in Waldorf education.

For many years there were only five established Waldorf schools in South Africa: two in Cape Town, one each in Johannesburg and Pretoria and one at Assegai near Hillcrest, kwaZulu/Natal. Four of these have high schools which prepare the students for the Matriculation examination. In recent years the focus has been on extending Waldorf education into black townships such as Soweto and Alexandra near Johannesburg, and Khayelitsha, Langa, Nyanga and Guguletu in Cape Town, as well as into rural areas. The provision by donors of resources not previously available for Waldorf teacher training led to new schools springing up, typically starting in garages or in small premises in rural areas.

Full-time Waldorf teacher training is conducted in both Cape Town and Johannesburg. In addition, more than 2000 teachers in State schools have been introduced to Waldorf education through teacher enrichment programmes operated by The Novalis Institute (see Appendix 1). The response of government school teachers to these imaginatively-based, independent programmes has been like rain falling on dry earth, and the demand for courses exceeds the availability of lecturers and funding. It is gratifying to hear participants on these courses testify to the validity and relevance of the methods and the renewing effect they have had on the teachers' sense of vocation. At the same time it is deeply disturbing to witness the extent to which an intellectually-based educational system is able to crush teachers' confidence and natural creativity, while for the children it means nothing less than the rich life and wonder of the world being reduced to mere information.

How is it Different?

There are many similarities and at the same time tremendous differences between a Waldorf classroom and a conventional one. Waldorf teachers believe that to educate the intellect alone is shortsighted and misleading. The world is filled with individuals who have received a good conventional education but who are racked by emotional and existential problems, or who have potential which they cannot use. Growing up in an increasingly complex world, they find that the "answers" they were taught at school do not stand them in good stead in finding their way in life. They often lack a sense of fundamental security and purpose and a real knowledge of the world and of themselves.

A crucial factor is that a purely intellectual education fails to sustain the pupil's interest. If the learning process is not alive, imaginative and filled with meaning through being related to the development of Man, the child is likely to lose interest and concentration and much teaching effort is simply wasted. This is especially so in the early school years, when children naturally expect the classroom to be filled with a sense of the wonder of the world. All too often, they simply receive information to process, as if they were already little adults working in a corporate or bureaucratic environment. As the Information Age continually generates more information to be processed, pressure feeds down from tertiary institutions into the secondary schools for a more rigorous school-leaving and university entrance examination, in keeping with the needs of industry and the academic world. This inevitably places more stress on the senior primary school, then on the junior primary and eventually the nursery school. Childhood is then in very real danger of being lost.

Waldorf schools have a unique curriculum which requires that learning be matched to the inner processes taking place within the child, which are largely observable through changes in physiological development. When one speaks about education as the development of the intellect alone one is speaking about one third of the human being — the head. Modern education is overwhelmingly directed at the development of the intellect. Rudolf Steiner speaks of the human being as a threefold physical being of head, heart and limbs, expressed in the form of the nerve-sense, rhythmic and metabolic systems of the body. He saw these as three interdependent physiological systems which are intimately integrated with, and serve as a basis for, the human qualities of thinking, feeling and willing respectively. Waldorf education recognises that the child develops these faculties in reverse order. In his earliest years, as any nursery school teacher or parent can attest, he is primarily a being of action, or will. As the nursery school years lay the foundation for healthy physical and emotional growth, the child develops his will through rhythmical activities involving language, drama, the celebration of seasonal festivals, baking, candle-making and so on.

By the change of teeth at six or seven years his feelings begin to develop in a more complex way, as the rhythmic system of heart and lungs, pulse and breathing, becomes the new focus of his physiological and psychological development. During this phase the essentially pictorial nature of the child's thinking, combined with a special receptivity in the child's feeling life at this stage, is the vehicle for acquiring knowledge in easily digestible ways. Last of all, around puberty, he acquires the ability to think objectively which is required of a mature adult. The young person now begins to learn more objectively through the thinking rather than through the feelings, and this need is best met by experiencing contrasting views of the world.

A Very Different View of the Child

This presents a very different view of the child from the stimulus-response model of the human being and the input-output model (however sophisticated) of much modern education. To a Waldorf teacher a child is not a highly-developed animal descended from apes. Rather, children are spiritual beings with a past, present and future, who need to be educated in freedom so that they can offer their gifts to the world when they are ready. Their faculties are precious and not to be force-fed to suit the vested interests of any political, industrial or educational system. The education is achieved by working imaginatively with the three seven-year periods of growth during which the child moves from infancy to adulthood. Because the inner nature of the child is qualitatively different during these periods, the methods used need to take account of this.

Much modern education has gone astray through attempts to "speed up" the process, by offering the child information at an increasingly earlier age. This implies that the intellectual ability of the child is the determining factor. It is, however, the child's overall inner readiness (including emotional readiness) that is all-important. In assessing this it must be recognised that the child's faculty of thinking develops more slowly than its will and feeling nature. There is therefore a great deal of information which the child has the intellectual ability to receive which it nevertheless would be disastrous for him to experience. As an example take the study of animals in a conventional primary school. This is often presented as abstract information in an impersonal way, leading ultimately to the dissection of a frog. At each step of the process the creature can be presented as a "thing" which the human being can use in any way, for any purpose, including that of scientific research. The approach is impersonal and therefore devoid of any moral component or sense of responsibility for the creature.

The Waldorf approach is always to relate the study of animals to the human being. In general the animal world as a whole is presented as containing the totality of the human being's animal nature, whereas the human is a synthesis of the specialised animal forms and functions. When teaching young children of nine or ten, the human faculties of thinking (seen as perception), feeling and willing could be presented as reflected respectively in the eagle with its exceptionally keen sight, the lion with its superb, harmonious, rhythmic system, and the cow, a miracle of metabolic processes which can turn grass into milk. Specifically, the cow, for instance, can be seen as an animal which serves the human being, producing milk and giving even her physical substance in the form of flesh and hide for human needs. A young child learning about the cow in this way would naturally feel both respect for and gratitude towards the animal. From the viewpoint of effective teaching, the Waldorf method is more effective: information conveyed via the intellect cannot but be superficial, since it is not being received by the whole of the child's nature. Warmed by the feelings through the child's emotional involvement, and expressed through action in the classroom, it is deeper and more powerful. It is also a moral education of which our societies are desperately in need. Most importantly, it respects the essentially reverent and wondering nature of the young child towards the world.

The Nursery School: Laying the Foundation.

These are the years when the young child's physical and emotional development are all-important. The will nature needs to be healthily expressed to foster the developing sense of self, social feelings and tolerance for others inculcated and the ground prepared for formal learning in a non-academic way. The child needs to become secure in his innermost being, confident about the world he lives in and his ability to cope with it. This is worth any amount of quick-start educational trickery. One is preparing the ground for the child's capacities to unfold and this need takes precedence over academic learning, which can be achieved more easily and quickly in the first primary school class when he is truly ready for it. It is significant that in the midst of apartheid Waldorf nursery schools have been places where children of all races have lived happily side by side, receiving an essential foundation for creative learning. In their small way, Waldorf kindergartens have been places where real foundations have been laid for social healing, preparing children from communities separated by apartheid for easy entrance to multiracial learning situations, while offering the some of the best quality education available.

The Primary School: Educating the Feelings

To say that Waldorf education during the primary school years accesses the learning process mainly through the feelings does not have anything to do with sentimentality. As a scientist, Rudolf Steiner was an intensely practical man who had no time for sentimentality of any kind and frequently warned against it. But the failure of so much well-intentioned education today has much to do with a fundamental misunderstanding about the way in which young children learn.

The young child lives in a world of inner mental pictures accompanied by a rich and strong emotional life. It is through this picture-consciousness that he should be educated because anything abstract and theoretical is death to his soul. Rudolf Steiner likened an overly intellectual approach to teaching to giving a young child a cold meal which is indigestible. The factual information must be warmed by the teacher's own humanity and set in the correct context in the light of his life experience. That is his purpose as a teacher — otherwise electronic media could do the job.

The work in the primary school is carefully designed to nourish the child at a deep level and to gradually stimulate his awakening intellect. Through painting, drawing, classroom plays, poetry, speech, movement, music and modelling, he will be privileged to explore a world many children unfortunately never experience — the world of the imagination. In the process he will develop capacities for living, rather than learn "answers" to questions which may never be asked. Those capacities, however, will enable the child to find his own answers to problems which may not yet exist during his growing up.

At each stage quality is stressed. In the early classes the literature content focuses not on dogs chasing balls, but on archetypal stories and legends which are meaningful and develop the child's moral life. Similarly, arithmetic is experienced as much more than learning to count and compute. Numbers appear in all their majesty as the foundation of the universe, with qualitative meanings. They are experienced physically through movement and visually as pattern drawings showing their unique characteristics. The number six, for instance is much more than four more than two. It is the difference between the two-ness of day and night, the four-ness of the seasons and the six-sidedness of a bee's home. History reveals the development of man's changing consciousness through the ages, while geography is a core subject teaching the brotherhood and inter-dependence of people. In every class and at every stage, children learn through the seven lively arts: drama, drawing, music, modelling, movement, painting and language. The lessons move through a combination of these, drawing the children into an imaginative world and enchanting them in the process.

The unique Waldorf main lesson system, pioneered 75 years ago, has influenced much modern thematic education. The first two hours of each day (the time when pupils are most alert) are used for periods of three to four weeks to teach a particular subject, enabling the children to explore the subject matter in depth and in a variety of ways. A three-level approach to teaching is used, in keeping with the threefold nature of the child's soul faculties of thinking, feeling and willing. The lesson usually begins with rhythmic activities such as recitation, singing and movement. This has a balancing effect, waking up the sleepy children and at the same time calming those of a nervous disposition. This method addresses the basic physical and emotional health of the pupil as a foundation for learning. Its effectiveness has frequently been noted in relation to those new pupils who have come to Waldorf schools clutching medical prescriptions, having been labeled "overactive" by teachers at their former schools where the learning was heavily intellectually based.

The second part of the main lesson builds on the "warming up" process described above and brings the intellectual content, the learning concepts. In the primary school classes this will be achieved mainly through the medium of stories with a strongly pictorial and imaginative character. First and second graders will relate best to nature study when the elements, plants and creatures speak to one another, for the young child lives into its surroundings in this way. Older primary school children will hear the stories as imaginative and scientifically accurate, but warmed by the teacher's loving interest in the world and in humanity. Teacher enrichment programmes based on these methods prove as nourishing for the trained State school teachers participating in them as they do for children and teachers in a Waldorf classroom. It is truly an education for life.

The High School: Finding Ideals and Identity

Secondary school takes the pupil from childhood, through puberty and adolescence to young adulthood. This is the third and culminating stage of schooling, when new-found capacities for argument, analysis and criticism become dominant; a time when the world and everything in it is subject to judgmental scrutiny, and either found wanting or adopted with idealistic fervour.

Crucial, during this phase, is the young person's discovery of gender. This is but one manifestation of the polarity that pervades existence. Whether or not the universe began with the creation of heaven and earth, light and darkness, or yin and yang, such polar division is fundamental to the world. Polarities become apparent at this age and their study forms a theme that runs through the high school curriculum: acids and bases in chemistry, poles in magnetism and electricity, idealism and corruption in sociology, orogenesis and erosion in geology. Such studies bring understanding to what has been learnt in the lower school: how the principles of expansion and contraction lead to the heat engine upon which the whole of today's industrial technology has been developed, how good and bad in the fairy tale became the modern motivation of political economy, and so on.

Thus, the classroom becomes relevant, not to the passing of examinations, but to life. The contrasts of character in literature, especially the Shakespearean plays, illustrate the richness of humanity in the world. The contrasts in black and white drawing done typically at the onset of puberty, illustrate the inner starkness of early adolescence. In such experiences, objective observation and personal awareness go hand in hand, and out of them grow the concepts and ideals of creative thought-life that is essential to the educational process at this age.

Both analytical and synthesizing thinking need to be experienced, the one showing the details and differences, the other the whole and the similarities. Most education stresses only the analytical — is it any wonder we are so much better at criticising than we are at creating? Preparing for life is much more than sitting for examinations. Becoming aware of one's identity as an individual is greatly helped by having the guidance of specialist teachers who see the young person above all, as a unique individual with a destiny to fulfil in community with his fellow human beings.

Such a view confirms the conviction which runs throughout Waldorf education — that the world is there for humankind and that everything in it has meaning only if it is related to individuals. It is only when the value of the individual is recognised that the rights of the community can be protected. Vaclav Havel's penetrating analysis shows that whatever political ideology is in vogue, a coldly intellectual evaluation of humanity will always run the risk of sacrificing the individual for vested political interests. It is very far from Rudolf Steiner's sober statement that every human life is infinitely precious because ultimately Man is "the religion of the gods."

We have entered deep waters — a living, conscious connection between God and the human being which focuses on the developing child as a gradually incarnating spiritual being. Seen from this perspective, an uncoordinated child in the first school class is not merely one with a psychomotor problem in its nerve-sense organism, but an individual with a spiritual core having difficulty in fitting into her body! The implications for education are shattering, for unless the spiritual heritage of our children is recognised they will be unable to find their way in human society. They will appear on the earth almost as lost souls, beings from another world finding it ever more difficult to relate to the increasingly alienating environment around them. They are utterly dependent on meeting parents and teachers who will "recognise" them in their inner spiritual nature, for this is the first step in any attempt to help them.

The theme of this article is that a new kind of education is needed because our civilisation is poised on the brink. What then, is the brink? Vaclav Havel has touched on it in his analysis of the fallen communist empire as an expedient, blinkered mechanical world view which excludes both a human and a spiritual reality. Interestingly, he has pointed to the capitalist world as being essentially no different, for it urges the human being to strive for material success: "Seek ye first the kingdom of earth ..." Alas, very little of real value can be "added unto" this success. Children educated narrowly to serve economic interests while their real needs as human beings are neglected, are beings whose souls are in prison and whose spirits have either been put to sleep or mechanised in the service of our technological world. Feeling trapped in a world devoid of morality or meaning, many are turning to drugs to find release. Drugs are the biggest symptom of the danger facing the children of the United States and many other Western nations — ironically, countries which have done most to provide an intellectually sound education.

We are beginning to see the consequences of excluding the education of the feeling life from our schooling. The drugs problem is such a consequence. It is not simply a criminal problem. The extreme ruthlessness of the drug dealers and the willingness of so many young children to seek drugs as an escape from the world we have created for them point to different outcomes from a similar source: these are indications that on the one hand, we have not been able to provide an education which is morally effective, while on the other hand current educational methods have totally failed to develop the courage and the inner resources needed to live in modern society.

The spirits of the children need to be awake so that they can develop their capacities for living and develop a love of learning, because what they are learning has meaning for them as growing human beings. In doing so they will also serve their country, for in the end it is the spiritual strength of a nation that enables it to survive. The brink on which we are standing is the abyss of materialistic thinking, which has created a world culture which is slowly but surely eliminating the spirit from human life — and without a spiritual dimension life has no meaning. All the thinkers we have quoted have expressed this in their different ways, but essentially they all agree on the nature of the crisis. It is probable that we will see this materialistic culture reaching its peak in the near future — indeed, the development of an extremely clever culture, in which to people who have been highly educated intellectually, spiritual concepts will appear quaint and amusing — perhaps even as symptoms in need of medical treatment, the way political dissidence has been seen under various dictatorships. If that day comes in its fullness we will indeed have "gained the world" — but at what cost?

4

DR RUDOLF STEINER — A "UNIVERSITY" IN HIMSELF

Stanford Maher

Almost 70 years ago, on March 30th, 1925, a man died in a sickbed which had been pulled to the foot of a huge 10-metre statue, on which he had worked until his energies ran out. The man was Dr Rudolf Steiner and the manner of his death, in that building in Dornach, Switzerland, symbolises the way in which he spent his life for the benefit of his fellow man.

The statue is significant, too. It shows a suffering figure striving to keep a balance between two others which represent extremes of idealism and rigidity. He gave it the curious name, "The Representative of Humanity".

Steiner died in his workshop on the site of a building which is today regarded as one of the most unusual pieces of architecture in the world. In his day it was revolutionary. The building which preceded it was even more remarkable. Made of wood, it was burned to the ground by critics hostile to the breakthroughs he was trying to achieve in several fields of knowledge.

If Rudolf Steiner achieved a fraction of what his followers claim for him, he may well be the greatest genius of the nineteenth and twentieth centuries, yet he is still relatively unknown. An extravagant claim — but how else can one describe a man who gave revolutionary ideas in education, medicine, science, art, religion, drama, psychology, architecture, economics, politics, and agriculture — impulses so powerful, that people working with them say they have hardly begun to tap their potential?

The experience of thousands of people working with those ideas in almost every country is that each year they become more relevant to the crises of the age. There is growing disenchantment today with what has been described as "the tyranny of the experts". More and more people are expressing reservations about issues such as the aridity of modern science, misuse of the earth, the bankrupt state of religion, and the "quality" of education in almost every advanced country.

Suspecting that a bogus intellectuality is replacing real creativity in many fields, they are interested in Steiner's unique insights, because this quiet, self-effacing Austrian showed ways in which a deeper understanding of man could be achieved and human culture renewed. Steiner was unimpressed by the modern over-emphasis on the intellect, regarding it as a kind of mental shorthand, the lowest level of thinking attainable by human beings, one which is "brainbound," because it is heavily influenced by the material nature of the body's nerve-sense organism.

Philosopher, scientist, dramatist, sculptor and artist, Steiner was as the German theologian and psychologist Friedrich Rittelmeyer observed, "a university in himself". His approach to knowledge astounded his contemporaries, who sometimes felt he was making claims which could not be tested scientifically. But his own life shows that he was no mystic, but a widely-read modern Western thinker, struggling to explain his perceptions of the underlying reasons for the crises facing humanity to the culture in which he lived.

He never tried to win converts and shunned theory, preferring to give of his talents in response to an immediate human need. So it is not surprising that the Waldorf school movement, today one of the largest independent educational movements in the world, came into being to meet the needs of the children of workers in a German cigarette factory. His famous methods of curative education, for which he is best known, stemmed from a personal experience. While working and studying in Vienna, Steiner tutored a retarded boy with a hydrocephalic condition, whose teachers declared him ineducable. Working intensively with his own methods, Steiner enabled the boy to attend grammar school and later to graduate as a medical doctor.

Rudolf Steiner was fully active in the literary, scientific and artistic movements of his day, both in Vienna and in Weimar, where he became a Goethe scholar. He was familiar with the writings of Marx and Engels. But in this field, as in others, he warned repeatedly against the "illusion" of attempting to find answers to human needs based on a purely materialistic view of man. Unless man's spiritual dimensions were rediscovered, the crises in the world would multiply, he said.

He was emphatic that this process of understanding anew the real nature of man was not to be sought through gurus, or by harping back to the wisdom of previous cultural epochs, but had to be achieved in a clear, conscious way by every individual, through heightened powers of thinking combined with healthy feeling.

In this sense he was perhaps akin to C G Jung, except that where Jung worked painstakingly through the depths of the unconscious, Steiner claimed from the beginning to have a clear perception of what is for others, unconscious human activity. Requests for his particular insights multiplied during his lifetime: doctors, priests, teachers, scientists, artists and academics asked him to show a way forward in fields which had become blocked by dogma of various kinds.

In his stance on the equality of women, he was far ahead of his time. Women were admitted as priests to the Christian Community, a non-denominational movement for religious renewal launched by priests who had turned to him for guidance. A humble man, who tackled problems of enormous significance. Who was he?

Steiner was born in Kraljevec, rural Austria, in 1861. The son of a railway station master, he grew up in the countryside, acutely sensitive to the natural forces around him. It is said that as a small child, he soon learned to distinguish between what was "seen" and what was "not seen" by adults. Unlike Wordsworth, who clearly remembered the loss of the special perceptions of childhood, Steiner was able to retain his own into adult life. This sense of wonder and enthusiasm is perhaps what imparts such an unusual quality to his learning. A gifted child, by the age of 15 he had rejected Kant's theory of human knowledge (which he had bound into the covers of his school history book) saying, "That may be true for him, but it is not true for me."

Kant had set boundaries to human knowledge, saying that man could never perceive reality, merely a picture of it. Steiner concluded on the basis of his own experience that there were no boundaries to knowledge, only to individual capacities to perceive it. There existed in every human being capacities of thought and feeling which could be developed to higher levels without escaping into mysticism, or forsaking the clarity of scientific thought, he declared.

"I believe that I possessed this knowledge in a form which can exist in consciousness with the same clarity that characterises mathematical knowledge", he later wrote. Throughout the 6000 lectures he gave during his lifetime — an average of one a day from 1902 until 1924 — Steiner emphasised man's ability to comprehend a spiritual reality underlying all of life.

Knowing was, for Steiner, the foundation on which the security of human beings was to be built in future decades, which he warned would include a dark age for human values. In particular, he forecast that the end of the 20th century would test the weaknesses of our civilisation. In lectures given in August 1919 (since published as a hard-hitting book, "Education as a Social Problem") he warned that human beings would face attempts to mechanise human thinking, vegetise human feeling and animalise the will — all three distortions of what he saw as being the three-fold nature of man's psychological make-up. He directed observers of the human condition to witness this happening in the United States, Europe and the Soviet Union respectively.

When still in his twenties he was invited to edit Goethe's natural scientific works. He discovered that he had independently arrived at the same world view as the great German poet and scientist: that direct, intuitive cognition of reality was possible. He maintained that this knowledge was real, not a subjective fantasy.

As a scientist, Steiner believed that scientific inquiry should be based on the methods and procedures of modern physical science. However, he was critical of a science which was preoccupied with measurement. He insisted that in the world of matter one could trace only effects, not causes, since the entire earth was and is a creation of spiritual beings. His research took him into areas which normal scientific inquiry does not reach. He developed his own path of knowledge, centred in a Christian world view, which he called Spiritual Science, or Anthroposophia: "Wisdom about the human being".

Steiner saw architecture as having an important influence on human beings. This most tangible of the arts was so important to him that just before World War

I, he built a unique building out of wood, the Goetheanum, named after the German poet and scientist he admired so much. The building, with its revolutionary idea of two enormous interlocking domes, was supported by giant pillars carved from different woods by craftsmen from many countries. He called it a "house of speech" and intended that it be filled with forms so artistic and imaginative, that visitors would be able to perceive as realities ideas which would be difficult to describe through lectures.

But his attempts to lead people to a more imaginative approach to the world's problems had aroused bitter enmity. The building was burned to the ground in an arson attack on New Year's Eve, 1922. Shaken but undeterred, he promptly started the building of another, this time from reinforced concrete, an innovation. It stands today on the site where the first Goetheanum stood, on a hill in Dornach, a village near Basel in Switzerland, where it houses the headquarters of the Anthroposophical Society.

Steiner's theory of education has created lasting interest, and has seen perhaps the greatest growth of all his ideas, giving birth to hundreds of independent "free schools" around the world. He saw education both as a science and as an art. Teachers had to understand both the spiritual soul life of the child, as well as the development of its intellect. Accordingly their task was to nourish the whole being of their pupils — to offer bread instead of stones by bringing a real experience of the world to children in an artistic creative way, rather than as indigestible lumps of information to be memorised for examinations.

He warned however against an unrealistic "progressive" approach in the classroom. Teaching in the primary school was to be based on the teacher's authority as an adult. The rhythm of the school day was to be based not on prescribed teaching schedules designed to suit a bureaucracy, but on the needs of the children. An artistic (and practical) approach to education would not prescribe specific lessons for each day of the year in advance, without knowing how the children would be thinking, feeling or willing at the time. Steiner insisted that only the teacher could know what her pupils needed on a particular day, and should have the freedom to act accordingly.

All the activities which have resulted from Steiner's influence are practised in South Africa, in one form or another. Schools for "normal" and for "handicapped" children exist (the gap between these definitions is closing year by year!), as do bio-dynamic organic farms. There is a wide range of people, from priests to businessmen, using his ideas, and doctors who practise an extended art of healing.

This article is a revision of one originally published in the Rand Daily Mail, Johannesburg, in 1982.

5

THE MOVEMENT THAT EVERYONE TRIES TO FORGET

John Davy O.B.E.

This article has been reproduced from The Times of London Educational Supplement, March 23rd, 1973. Only the statistics have been updated.

Some 450 000 pupils attend the one thousand-odd Rudolf Steiner schools all over the world. They are all fully comprehensive co-educational, unstreamed schools taking normal children from kindergarten to eighteen. (They are quite distinct from the many homes and schools for handicapped and maladjusted children and adults run on Steiner lines.) The movement is strongest in Germany, where the first Waldorf School was founded in Stuttgart in 1919 for the children of employees of the Waldorf-Astoria cigarette factory. The German schools were closed by the Nazis, but reopened in 1945, and now number more than 30. The movement has spread to most European countries, as well as to the United States, Canada, Australia, New Zealand, South Africa and South America.

The thirty schools in Britain which form the Steiner Schools Fellowship feel themselves somewhat out on a limb in their own country. They are all growing, or at least holding their own, in spite of severe economic pressures. They have no endowments, and none of the snob appeal which attracts wealth. Nor do they promise high-octane A level performance. Their examination results are adequate in relation to an entry which is not selected on academic ability, but the specialist demands of the British examination system have forced serious distortions of the kind of work which the schools really want to nurture in their senior classes, and no-one is fully satisfied with the resulting compromise. Yet interest grows. There is a steady stream of visitors and inquiries. The teachers themselves have a pressing sense of the relevance of their ideals and practices to many current educational conundrums. Nevertheless, the schools were never intended to become the preserve of a mainly middle-class minority which can pay fees. So they are asking themselves, with some urgency, what place this kind of education will be able to find in Britain in the next few years.

Not many educationists or teachers in this country know much about Steiner education. This is partly the fault of the movement itself. There is very little literature in English, and Steiner teachers have been too busy to spend much time making their work more widely known. There are, though, some other obstacles. The somewhat empirical temper of British cultural life means that most practising teachers approach their work as a craft, and — often wisely — distrust theories and systems. But Steiner's aim was to found an education on a detailed understanding of child development — and his account of this development quickly leads beyond the usual frames of reference in which most people are accustomed to discuss these matters.

This means that whoever begins to study Steiner's work seriously will quickly be led into deep waters. He may begin to scent whiffs of what seems like mysticism or occultism, and he will certainly need to make some relationship with the extraordinary figure of Steiner himself. People may come to terms fairly easily with someone who claims to speak, as Steiner did, out of direct spiritual experiences, so long as he or she pronounces mainly about some other world, or about religions or inner matters safely insulated from practical life. It is different when such a person begins to describe his activities as spiritual research and to bring the results to bear on such humdrum problems as the teaching of arithmetic.

Steiner himself who, as a young man had many friends among leading artists, philosophers and scientists in Vienna, Weimar and Berlin before the turn of the century, was largely ostracised by his circle from the moment he began to speak directly of his personal spiritual experience. Yet he did not begin to do so until he had, at least to his own satisfaction, fully understood the relationship of this experience to the familiar functioning of the human mind in thought, feeling and action, and had formulated this as a clear theory of knowledge which he published first as a doctoral thesis (Truth and Science) and soon afterwards enlarged and developed, as a book (The Philosophy of Freedom).

Practical Renewal

Nevertheless, it was another 20 years before he began to be approached seriously by teachers, doctors, farmers, scientists and others, asking not merely for help in their personal lives but for a renewal in their practical work. (During this period he lectured and taught, at first mainly to members of the German Theosophical Society, and later within the Anthroposophical Society which he founded in 1913. This led to work in drama and the arts.) To his work with the first group of teachers in Stuttgart after World War I Steiner also brought a certain amount of teaching experience of his own. He had not worked in a classroom but, coming from a very poor Austrian family, he had to work to support himself, while studying for a science degree at Vienna's Technical University, by extensive private tutoring.

Steiner wished the Waldorf schools to be judged by their work. He intended them to be, quite simply, good schools. Waldorf teachers are not expected to inculcate a particular world outlook into their pupils but to equip them to find their own ways as adults. Of course the phrase "good school" begs a lot of questions, which, if they are pursued at all, quickly become very large questions indeed. Few people who think seriously about education would measure the real value of a school's work by its examination results or by the income and social status of its pupils in later life. What matters is whether pupils go on to realise their full potential and make fruitful relationships with others. Success, in these terms, is barely measurable. Nevertheless, as a general statement of aims, this would apply well enough to Steiner schools. But for teachers and educationists the significance of this form of education must lie not in such generalities but in the details of concepts and practice.

What is the basis of a school curriculum? Why do we teach what we teach? The simplest answer is that an educated person should have acquired certain knowledge (the "subjects" of established school tradition) and learnt certain skills (notably the three Rs). Fortunately this is seldom satisfactory today. We know that the conventional subjects, treated simply as bodies of knowledge, lead all to easily to the aridities of chalk-and-talk, to boredom and deserts of abstraction. The selection and teaching of skills no longer seems such plain sailing either. The behavioural sciences are beginning to offer more powerful techniques for training and shaping behaviour — but this is making us aware that all training embodies certain social and moral assumptions. The radical response is that all education is a device for perpetuating various kinds of tyranny. Between these two extremes there has grown the search for a truly child-centred education, a search in which all Steiner teachers also feel themselves to be most deeply engaged. To this search, Steiner made two main contributions: first, a detailed account of child development (many features of which have subsequently been confirmed and supplemented by the work of Piaget, Gesell *et al*) and second, an approach to a curriculum designed to support this development which is still, in its conception and detail, unique.

It is characteristic that Steiner emphasised the physical development of the child as much as the psychological. This accounts for the emphasis on chronological age, as opposed to developmental age, which often surprises visitors to Steiner schools. Yet it would be strange, unless we really believed in the Cartesian dichotomy divorcing mind wholly from matter, if the maturation of the organism were not linked with maturation of the mind.

Children, Steiner said, do not grow up — they "grow down", from head to limbs. And as they grow down physically, they wake up, psychologically, from limbs to head. The new-born baby is all head; the limbs are more or less appendages. The adolescent, by contrast, often goes through a stage when he seems to be all limbs, before reaching final adult proportions.

Place Of Authority

Yet waking up proceeds, in a sense, in the opposite direction. Babies and nursery-age children learn mainly by doing (Piaget's *sensori-motor* and Bruner's *enactive* stage of development). Not until adolescence does the individual begin to use his head in an adult way, when he becomes capable of more abstract intellectual operations, as well as devastating criticism and analysis of his surroundings.

During the all-important middle years — which Steiner placed explicitly between two stages of physical maturation, change of teeth and puberty — the inner and outer growth processes cross, so to speak, in the heart of childhood. The rhythms of pulse and breathing begin to approach the adult's, movements become more rhythmic and graceful, and the child is for a while beautifully balanced until the awkwardness of adolescence begins. At the same time, a rich inner life of imagination, fantasy and feeling begins to unfold — everything becomes heartfelt.

For Steiner, this was not a mere figure of speech. He regarded the rhythmic functions of the body, which are embodied most explicitly in the heart and lungs, as the organic basis of our emotional life, as the limbs are the basis for action and the brain for thought. Thus while the pre-school child lives essentially in the immediate events around him, the seven-year-old begins to dispose of a freer life of imagination and feeling, with which he can enter into painting, story-telling or games in a new way. At this time, thought is not naturally critical and analytic, but pictorial and dramatic. The stories enjoyed by under-fives are mainly a series of happenings; but then there begins to awaken a sense for stories filled with drama, triumph and tragedy, laughter and tears, good and evil, and a meeting of reality with mystery and magic.

For this stage of childhood Steiner wanted teachers above all to work as artists, not to teach art as a subject, but to bring into classroom activities all the living imagery, colour, poetry and magic of which they are capable. Classroom practice, too, should have a living organic balance between listening, speaking, doing, between humour and seriousness, impulse and patience, taking in, transforming and giving out. To work with children in this way, to learn to know them as a social group and take account of individual needs, demands a great deal of time.

This led Steiner to recommend that each class in the junior school should have a class teacher, who moves up the school with the group, spends at least two hours of each day with them, and is responsible for a substantial part of their work for the eight years from six to 13 (although languages, games, eurythmy, crafts, etc., may be taken by specialist teachers). This is obviously a great challenge and a great opportunity for the teachers concerned. They are not bound by a strict timetable, and can shape the work to the needs and progress of their group. Thus for nearly 75 years they have had in their classrooms the flexibility and scope which the more progressive primary schools in this country are now attempting to establish.

But Steiner recommended the class teacher system for a further reason, which seems at first less in tune with the times. Maturation from the infant to adult includes, Steiner said, a development in the child's natural relation to authority. The small child is essentially imitative, and is supported above all by security and routine. The adolescent is essentially critical, and is best guided on the one hand by reason, on the other by integrity. But in the middle years, Steiner insisted, the child expects and needs authority, not didactic or autocratic, but the chance to repose confidence in an adult as a source of wisdom and guidance. It is the relationship which led adults in other cultures and other times to expect authoritative guidance from the elders of a family or tribe.

Sources Of Knowledge

The crucial experience for children at this stage, Steiner insisted, is not knowledge as such, but how knowledge lives in individual human beings. The chilly notion of impersonal truth, which stems from the sciences (and is now being recognised there for the dangerous myth that it is), is quite foreign to childhood. It comes quite naturally to an eight-year-old to expect his teacher to know almost everything. He brings an instinct and capacity for trust which can be a precious gift for later life, and feels betrayed by the adult who offers only scepticism and self-doubt. When an eight-year-old is encouraged to "find out for yourself", often by reference to books and films, the implication is that these impersonal resources for learning have an authority which the living human being lacks.

This is not to say that children in Steiner schools are never encouraged to look up things or make use of books. But such work takes second place to the sharing of first-hand experience and exploration between teachers and children. By moving up the school with his class, the teacher is having to grow constantly himself, and from his enthusiasm and energy for this work there can flow the natural authority which Steiner hoped for, an authority of a life's work, not of a dead hand.

With puberty, a new relationship is needed. The adolescent begins to have a more detached and critical view of the adults around him, but can recognise and respect authority based on mastery of different fields of work. In the upper school, therefore, pupils work with specialist teachers, although the format of a main lesson, lasting two hours a day in block periods of four or five weeks, is retained. This allows all pupils to follow a broad curriculum of common studies in humanities and sciences until 18 (although in Britain, the demands of A level work compel much modification of the programme in the sixth form).

Perhaps the most interesting field for detailed study by teachers and educationists are the suggestions Steiner made, not only for the general approach to different age groups, but for the actual content of the curriculum to support successive stages of development. To appreciate Steiner's thinking here, it is necessary to look more closely at his view of these.

As already mentioned, Steiner emphasised chronological age as much as mental age. The physical development of the child is looked after by nature; the doctor intervenes mainly to correct conditions of imbalance caused by illness or malnutrition. Children in advanced countries now grow bigger and come into puberty earlier than a century ago. (Whether this is in any way an advantage is disputable. We can be thankful for the disappearance of deficiencies caused by too little good food, but they are in danger of being replaced with disorders caused by too much bad food.)

However, it is accepted that there is a normal path of physical development from birth to adult, which is fairly constant. A proposal to manipulate this development, for example by inducing puberty at five, would not find much support. A long maturation process is clearly associated with the unique capacities of the human species.

In a competitive society, though, in which there is a premium on certain kinds of intellectual skills, psychological maturation is often viewed differently. Although it is somehow linked with physical maturation, it appears to be rather more mobile and malleable, so that under-fives may be trained to perform what look like adult intellectual feats (not only reading and writing, but various logical and mathematical operations). At the same time, the crucial and formative nature of the pre-school years has increasingly impressed child psychologists, with the result that a growing weight of educational research and technology is beginning to focus on the nursery and even on the cradle. Steiner was emphasising the extreme importance of the first five years of life, more than 75 years ago. This arose from his view that this first stage of development is dominated essentially, by imitation in a very fundamental sense of the word.

Time Factor

The distinction between "I" and "the world", which adults take as given, awakens only gradually. The infant, Steiner said, at first experiences himself as inwardly and outwardly united with all that happens around him. He should, for example, be surrounded by rich and well-formed human speech, irrespective of whether he understands all that he hears. But it does not follow that this openness should be exploited to achieve precocious performance of specialised forms of behaviour currently valued by adults, and to do so, Steiner claimed, might seriously impoverish other aspects of development (even leading, much later in life, to physical and constitutional weaknesses).

Behind Steiner's approach to this question lies a view of the human being which goes right outside the usual framework of educational discussion. For he regarded growing up as the gradual incarnation of an individual human spirit into a psychological organism, and education as essentially concerned to support this incarnation process. And the gradual maturation of new faculties and modes of awareness he regarded as intimately linked with the process of growing into various functions of the organism, as these themselves mature.

Thus during infancy the human being is growing especially into his digestive and metabolic functions, and is nourished by every aspect of his surroundings as directly as by his food. After the change of teeth, he is growing more particularly into the rhythmic organs of heart and lungs, which awakens an inner experience swinging between expansion and contraction, laughter and tears, and brings a relationship to the world which is neither imitative unity nor detached observation, but a consciousness which has some of the drama and variety of vivid dream.

Then at adolescence, according to Steiner, the human spirit begins to unite itself more deeply with the parts of the organism which are, so to speak, nearest to death — with the functions of nerves and senses, and with the skeleton. Out of this grow at their proper time the adult's capacities for detachment, clear observation and objective thought.

This account of childhood needs to be looked at in conjunction with Steiner's view of history. He did not accept the notion that human beings of earlier cultures shared the same detached apprehension of nature as ourselves, while simply entertaining more confused theories which they then projected as myths. He regarded these mythologies rather as entirely valid descriptions of real experience, associated with a different mode of consciousness.

What we know as our modern consciousness is essentially a dualistic apprehension of ourselves *vis-a-vis* the world (and which generates nowadays varying degrees of alienation). This began to awaken, according to Steiner, among the Greek philosophers, and more generally in Europe with the Renaissance. Modern science was born out of just that sense of detachment which gradually overtakes each modern child around adolescence. Behind the historical development, too, according to Steiner, we should learn to see a gradual process of incarnation of the human spirit.

This is the essential background out of which Steiner began to make suggestions for building a school curriculum — a curriculum through which the organic process of becoming at home in the body can go hand-in-hand and be supported by an education which leads the human being to be at home in the world. There is space here only to pick out a few examples.

With the younger children, Steiner urged teachers wherever possible to proceed from the whole to the part, from living to non-living, from action to knowledge, from man to nature. Thus writing precedes reading in Waldorf schools, and the former will emerge out of imaginative experience and action. For example, before introducing the letter W, the teacher may tell a sea story full of wind and waves. The children will act waves, learn a watery, wavy poem, and paint waves. Out of the painting, the teacher will lead into a more formal exercise of the letter form — an abstraction, but one born out of a living experience. The child thus follows, essentially, the same process as the historical development of writing, from pictograms to our present skeletal but convenient alphabet.

The children will also both hear and speak many stories and poems in their own language, and in at least one foreign language (more often two), before there is much emphasis on solitary reading and writing. The music and rhythm of words are important experiences for young children, as most parents know, long before their meaning is fully grasped.

Throughout the first school years, the children's imaginative life and grasp of language will be nourished by hearing, re-telling, acting and illustrating stories. For the six-year-olds the teacher may draw mainly on fairy stories, moving on at seven to fables and legends, to Old Testament stories at eight, Norse stories and sagas at nine, Greek myths and legends at 10. In using a sequence of this kind, the teacher leads children through different qualities of imaginative experience, gradually "down to earth", preparing the way for history proper.

By the eleventh year, children have begun to have a sense of time more like the adult's, while the intellect has become more awake and critical. At this time, Steiner suggested, teachers could introduce Greek history, which begins as myth and ends as fact, while Greek culture and consciousness move from mythology through philosophy, and prepare the way for the more prosaic world of Rome.

It is generally recognised that the first experiences of arithmetic are crucial, and here Steiner made some interesting recommendations. By starting with "two plus two equals four", the child meets (i) a completely abstract proposition, (ii) a reductionist view of the universe in which wholes are made up of parts, and (iii) a problem with only one answer. If he explores instead how to divide an apple or a cake and share it round the class, he starts from real life, from wholeness, and from a problem with several answers. Similarly, the teacher may first introduce children to Roman numerals, in which II arises by dividing the wholeness of I, instead of launching straight into the Arabic system with its powerful but highly abstract concept of zero. The children will also find their way into number through old-fashioned chanting of tables, as well as through musical rhythms and stepping games. As in so much else, at this age the children need to learn by heart before they learn by head.

The way into the sciences also follows a gradual path from imagination to observation and abstraction. For six-year-olds it seems perfectly natural for animals, plants and rocks to talk to each other, as well as humans. By the ninth year, though, there comes an important transition on which Steiner placed much stress (in Gesell's account, this age marks the emergence of "self-motivation"). One symptom is moments of sudden private loneliness, feelings of detachment from parents and home, often coupled with sudden rebellion. It can be like a premature glimpse of adolescence. To weather this crisis, the child needs to become at home in the world in a new way.

Here Steiner suggested that the children should come to know various forms of human work where craft, skill and knowledge of materials and the environment are important — the farmer, fisherman, builder, blacksmith. The children may churn butter, build a wall, and perhaps, if they can find a cooperative farmer, cut and bind a small amount of wheat before the impersonal combine harvester takes over. A period on house-building can include many realistic exercises in plan-making, calculation of areas and quantities.

Drugs and Tolkien

Many schools embark on elaborate projects of this kind nowadays, with most valuable results. But the notion that house-building, in particular, has a special value in the ninth year must seem abstract and strange without some appreciation of the child's inner situation at this time — his need to make himself at home in the world and in his body in a new way. Steiner suggested that this period could be accompanied by a first introduction to formal grammar, to the construction and building-bricks of language. Here again Steiner teachers will tend to start with activities (the verbs) before going on to things (the nouns).

From the crafts and trades, the class will probably move on, in the tenth year, to local history and geography, including first exercises in map-making (for example, a detailed representation of the way from home to school). Gradually, the children move from their immediate human environment into natural history and the sciences, beginning with the kingdom closest to man, the animals.

Here Steiner recommended teachers to start with studies of the form and ways of life of some characteristic higher animals — eagle, mouse, lion, cow, octopus, etc. In particular, he hoped that children would experience the specialised adaptations of such animals in relation to the versatile and in many respects unspecialised form of man. Next will come botany, introducing more emphasis on careful observation of the surroundings, and some first discussion of ecological questions (Steiner was already emphasising the importance of educating children to care for the earth in 1919). Geography will expand beyond the locality to take in, for example, a whole region or continent, and in their twelfth year, the class will begin to look at climate, meteorology, astronomy, mineralogy, to awaken gradually a sense for the life and structure of the earth within a wider universe.

As puberty approaches, the physical sciences are first introduced more formally. Steiner anticipated a good deal of modern thinking about science teaching in recommending that a strong element of observation and discovery should precede theoretical explanation. But he also, less fashionably, urged that the artistic experience of earlier classes should not be banished from the laboratory, but welcomed. Thus Steiner teachers may begin physics with acoustics, which can be introduced through music, the making and tuning of bamboo pipes and demonstrations of the remarkable forms on a vibrating Chladni plate. Likewise, an exploration of the phenomenology of colour (including, for example, after-images, coloured shadows and other phenomena usually better known to artists and psychologists than to physicists) will precede optics.

The great changes which overtake young people at puberty are familiar enough, and do not need to be rehashed here. Many teachers probably share Steiner's hope for a final four years of schooling to help the emerging individual find and test his own powers of discrimination and judgment in relation to every aspect of modern life, an education for freedom. A great many of the difficulties of adolescence have to do with inner and outer unfreedoms, and here Steiner predicted that the effects of environmental and educational inadequacies in earlier years would at this age begin to make themselves sharply felt.

The imitative needs of the infant, if not appropriately met, can re-emerge at puberty and make the adolescent helplessly vulnerable to every passing fashion. And the natural need of the first school years to look up to some adults with affection and confidence as trustworthy authorities, if not adequately fulfilled, can manifest in the adolescent as over-dependence or indiscriminate worship of cult heroes.

Steiner also emphasised the enormous importance of sustaining work in the arts and crafts right up to school leaving age as the most essential help for adolescents struggling to integrate their turbulent new life of feeling and will with an awakening critical intellect. A number of features of adolescent culture which have become familiar since Steiner's time seem to confirm his warnings of the trouble which imaginative deprivation and over-intellectualisation in early school years would bring. (Is it possible that in turning to drugs and Tolkien, teenagers may in part be attempting to make good a lack of fairy stories in infant school?)

Evolving Individuals

There is no space here to describe Steiner's many suggestions for the last four years of schooling, which he held should be available to every young person, whatever their academic abilities. Conditions in the world are very different from the Stuttgart of 1920 and particularly in Germany, some Steiner schools have recently inaugurated interesting experiments in secondary education, notably attempts to combine continued liberal studies and artistic work with industrial apprenticeships and various forms of craft and vocational training.

In Britain (one of the few European countries where Steiner schools get no state aid), such developments are unfortunately blocked at present. School-centred apprenticeships do not fit into the British scheme of things, while the highly specialised academic demands of A levels are quite foreign to the broad experience of many aspects of the real world which Steiner wanted. The current doubts about A level specialisation and the whole pattern of higher education may gradually lead to a situation in which the British Steiner schools will be able to realise more of their full potential.

There is not space here either to describe Steiner's account of the four "temperaments" in children and adults which the teacher should learn to recognise, nor to go into his recommendation that each school should be run by a community or college of teachers, without a headmaster. In the relatively short time in which Steiner worked with the first Waldorf school, before his death in 1925, he produced a great wealth of suggestions, many of which have still to be fully tested and worked out.

Ultimately what matters about Steiner education is not only whether the schools work, but whether the premises on which they are based are true. Much of what Steiner was saying about child development in 1919 now looks remarkably prescient in the light of work done since. But his account of the meaning of this development is still barely discussible in polite intellectual society. Educational debate tends to skirt round the central question of the essential nature of the human individual. Steiner teachers build all their work round a conviction that each pupil is the bearer of an evolving human spirit with a past and a future leading beyond birth and death. It is not a fashionable view in a sceptical age. But it brings a natural sense of affinity with all other teachers — and luckily there are quite a number — for whom education means caring for the essential humanity of each individual as it emerges and matures in every child.

6

EDUCATING FOR CREATIVE THINKING: The Waldorf Approach To Educational Problems In The United States

Joan Almon

Old solutions are not adequate for modern problems. Their solution requires a renewal of thinking, and there is no better starting point for that renewal than with the education of children, especially young children. Educators generally agree that the quality of thinking among American students has been deteriorating at the very time when modern life needs more creativity and liveliness in human thought. In this article, I will explore some aspects of the development of creative thinking and some of the ways in which Waldorf education works to cultivate it among its students.

Thinking and the Goals of Waldorf Education

Although Waldorf Education originated over seventy years ago, many people believe it will show its full promise in the twenty-first century rather than in the twentieth. The fact that it has been undergoing rapid growth all around the world since 1970, and that the growth rate is accelerating in the 1990s, indicates that it may well be an education now coming into its own because it fosters a thinking appropriate for our age.

At the same time, many other forms of education are under increasing attack. American public schools, for example, are facing a crisis in thinking, and educators everywhere are trying to understand why. There are three key manifestations of the crisis, as has been reported in the media and discussed at educational conferences. At the pre-school level, many children are showing signs of stress and are not doing well in academically oriented kindergartens. Educators are now recommending a return to a play-oriented curriculum in the kindergarten, rather than the academic one that has prevailed for the past twenty years. At the elementary school level, one frequently hears about burnout among third- and fourth-grade pupils. After age nine, many children simply do not want to learn any more. In the high school, educators say that many students seem unable to think. Ask them a defined question that requires a true/false answer or a multiple choice, and they do all right. But ask them to think through a problem and explain their solutions, and many are at a loss. Few educators seem to see a relationship between these three crises, but, from a Waldorf point of view, the problems of the elementary school and high school follow on the heels of the early emphasis given to academics in the kindergartens as surely as night follows day. The high school situation is of particular concern to American society, which is looking for an acceleration in thinking but is finding instead a decay. The educational community is deeply concerned over how to "teach thinking" to its students. The crisis in thinking is well described by Jane Healy, an educator whose interest is brain research and the development of the mind. In her book Endangered Minds (1990), she writes:

"'Teaching thinking skills', another 'movement' currently passing through the education system, is a response to a growing concern that Johnny can't think any better than he can read. Programmes attempting to teach thinking skills are selling like hotcakes at teachers' conferences and workshops. Yet critics scornfully point out it is a contradiction in terms to rely on packets, workbooks, computer drills, and worksheets to engage students' higher cognitive abilities."

Healy goes on to point out the need for two types of mental activity in the students if they are to be well-developed thinkers: the analytic and the creative.

"Good thinking requires good analytic skills, but it also depends on imagination. Both halves of the brain, not simply the linear, analytic-verbal left hemisphere, contribute to it. The more visual, intuitive right hemisphere probably provides much of the inspiration, while the left marches along in its dutiful role as timekeeper and realist ... Some observers, concerned about declines in creative thinking, as well as in imagination, have advocated teaching methods and classroom experiences to stimulate the right hemisphere ... (but) it is increasingly clear that genuine creative imagination springs from much deeper developmental roots — which can easily get short-changed in homes and in schools."

It is these deeper developmental roots of creative thinking that have interested me greatly as a Waldorf educator of young children. Analytic thinking is a very important aspect of thought in modern life and needs to be cultivated, along with the creative side of thinking. But because it is already so valued by modern society, I will only touch on it lightly in this article, although much could be said about how to integrate it into a creative curriculum. The focus will be on the other half of thinking, the creative, imaginative side. Under present social circumstances, there is a great danger that the creative aspect of the mind will atrophy under the onslaught of the media, of the hours spent in dry academic studies, and of the pressure produced by standardised exams. If we can help children to grow up with both sides of the mind actively maturing, then new forms of thought are possible, forms that are much needed now and in the future. It is clear that creative, multi-disciplinary approaches to learning will be necessary if we are to solve major problems such as environmental issues. There is much talk about divergent thinking as an appropriate form for the future. Such thinking is defined as "creative, imaginative and flexible thinking that results in a variety and abundance of ideas or answers to a problem" (Thesaurus 1990, 72). Parents and educators remark that they commonly find such thinking in Waldorf graduates.

As a young teacher in the early 1970s, I was committed to being very eclectic in my approach to education. Some friends and I started a nursery school whose primary goal was to keep the spirit of the child lively and growing. We had all experienced the deadening effects of our own education and were convinced that there must be a better way to keep the inner spark of the child alive. When we first discovered Waldorf education, we liked the ideas and the methods, but it was really the children who convinced me that this education brought them more deep-seated satisfaction than any of the other approaches that we offered them. As we brought more Waldorf ideas into the classroom, the children turned to them and drank them in deeply. They opened to them like flowers opening to the sun. Their responses went well beyond their enjoyment of other educational practices that we offered them. The children convinced me that they loved Waldorf education, but I had many questions worked over the long run. What sort of thinking did the students display in high school? How did they do in college? How did they do in life? For years, I plagued the more experienced Waldorf teachers with my questions.

One Waldorf high school teacher told a story that made a deep impression on me. When her high school was new, it encouraged its twelfth graders to apply to less-pressured colleges, steering them towards small liberal arts schools. Gradually, the school's confidence grew, and it began to encourage students to apply to Ivy League schools. A number were accepted and, in their first year there, letters from the colleges began to arrive at the school, saying, "Send us more of your students. They are not necessarily the most intellectual students we have had, but they are by far the most well-rounded."

These thoughts are echoed by other educators who have worked with Waldorf graduates. For example, Dr. Warren Eickelberg (1991), professor of biology and director of the premedical curriculum at Adelphi University, has worked with a number of Waldorf graduates. He has this to say about them:

"Without any doubt my past three decades (in the teaching profession) have been marked by change, and ever more change. Throughout this dynamism of activity, where values were under attack and standards of behaviour were challenged, from time to time there would be a unique stabilising influence in my classes: a Waldorf School graduate. And they were different from the others. Without exception they were, at the same time, caring people, creative students, individuals of identifiable values, and students who, when they spoke, made a difference.

"Waldorf School graduates see behind the facts that often must be repeated or explained on examination. They are keenly interested in the macrocosm of the universe and microcosm of the cell's ultrastructure, but they know that Chemistry,

Biology and Physics can't tell them much about the nature of love. I feel certain that all Waldorf School graduates believe in the orderliness of our universe, and they believe the human mind can discern this order and appreciate its beauty."

Another quotation indicates that it is not only at the college level that the Waldorf students' thinking capacities shine forth. In Marin County, California, the Waldorf school goes only to eighth grade, and students transfer to local high schools, private and public, for the remainder of their schooling. A number have attended the Marin Academy, and its history teacher, James Shipman (1991) describes them in this way:

"What I find most remarkable about Waldorf kids (is that) they have been taught to think: thinking is an "okay" activity for them to engage in. I think they intrinsically understand the difference between thinking about an issue and merely memorising "the right answer" for the test ... It is as if somewhere in their early years of schooling they somehow got the idea that learning is a lifelong enterprise."

These anecdotal remarks describe some of the qualities of Waldorf students. There are not yet many quantitative studies about Waldorf education, but one major study in Germany compared Waldorf graduates with those graduating from college preparatory high schools called Gymnasia. Professors at the University of Bonn studied the test scores of 1460 Waldorf students on the very rigorous state college entrance exam, the Abitur. The study compared their scores with those of students attending Gymnasia. The expectation was that Gymnasia students would score higher than the Waldorf students because the whole of the state school curriculum is geared towards the Abitur, but the opposite was found. Not only did the Waldorf school students score better than Gymnasia students, but the longer the students had been in a Waldorf school, the higher they scored (*Der Spiegel*). While the Abitur is hardly a test of creative thinking, these results do show that Waldorf education, far from handicapping students who prepare for such tests, actually seems to help them do well.

A Threefold View of the Human Being

What is it about Waldorf education that cultivates such all-around human qualities, including a strong capacity for thinking? When Rudolf Steiner founded the first Waldorf School, he placed much emphasis on three activities of the human soul — thinking, feeling, and willing. Steiner related these three aspects with the major parts of the physical body. He associated thinking with the brain and nervous system, feeling with the heart and lungs, which he called the rhythmic system, and will activity with the limbs and metabolic system.

The three areas are distinct but also highly interconnected. One cannot function without the other two, yet each brings its unique qualities to the individual. When we speak of a well-balanced person, we usually mean that all three aspects are active and working together harmoniously. If one aspect predominates so strongly that others are suppressed, we find one-sided people. From this condition there arise stereotypes and caricatures. The caricature professor, for example, lives in an ivory tower, a picture of living solely in the activity of thinking, isolated from feelings and will. In contrast, the oversized jock, all brawn and no brain, lives in the will, in the limbs and in the huge amounts of food he consumes. In between, the artist is wrapped up in the feeling life, a bohemian existence teeming with human relationships and with little connection to the practical or intellectual. These are extremes, of course, but the pictures are helpful in understanding how one-sided we become if we do not cultivate all three aspects of our nature.

Rudolf Steiner not only described the three aspects in rich detail but spoke of how to educate children in order to develop all three capacities. Thinking, feeling, and willing do not develop at identical rates, but rather the focus is first on one, then on another. In the first seven years of life, the child is primarily living in the will, learning nearly everything through physical activity. During these years, learning takes place mostly in an unconscious manner through the child's imitation of the activities of adults and older children. Between the approximate ages of seven and fourteen, the child's feeling life is the strongest, and all that is taught through imagination and the arts penetrates deeply. Human relationships are also of great importance at this age. In a Waldorf school, they are fostered through the relationship with the class teacher, who ideally remains with the class for eight grades, teaching all the main lesson subjects and developing a deep connection with the children and their families. It is also very important that, in addition to creativity and imagination, the teacher foster an orderliness and healthy respect for boundaries in the classroom. These qualities will emerge later in the students' thinking, as well.

In the high school, cognitive and intellectual thinking awaken strongly, and students now work with teachers who are specialists in their own subjects. The students are helped to observe phenomena, especially in the sciences, so that they can formulate their own conclusions and learn to explain and defend them. The thrust is toward developing independent judgment in the students, rather than feeding them finished statements. By working with diverse points of view in their studies, the students become skilled in looking at questions from a number of sides and appreciating the differences that are uncovered.

When the thinking in the high school years builds upon the feeling in the grade-school years and upon the will fostered in the pre-school age, the result is a mind characterised by creative imagination (thinking plus feeling), coupled with a strong wish to bring ideas down into practical reality (thinking plus will). It is a mind that sees relationships between the sciences or the world of nature on the one side and the humanities or the world of mankind on the other. It enjoys the interpenetration of the two. Such a mind also sees human activity, including thinking, as a harmonious art of a greater universal picture. The cultivation of such a world view is an essential element of Waldorf education.

From early childhood on, a sense of wonder, gratitude, and reverence is cultivated in the child. He sees himself as part of a greater universe in which the hand of the creator plays a mighty role. Waldorf education is not a religious education in the sense of teaching a religion, but Rudolf Steiner (1979, 14) spoke often of the sense of wonder in childhood and the importance of cultivating it as a precursor to thinking. He described it in this way: "It is absolutely essential that before we begin to think, before we so much as begin to set our thinking in motion, we experience the condition of wonder." Although they are not affiliated with any religious institution, the Waldorf schools are filled with a deep reverence for the divine aspects of life. The human being is viewed as a bridge between the heavenly and earthly realms of life, and Waldorf education makes room for both realms.

Laying a Foundation for Creative Thinking

The development of thinking is a rich and complex story, and one can only give a brief introduction to it in an article of this length. I have chosen to focus primarily on the first seven years of childhood for two reasons. One is that early childhood has been the focus of my own work for the past twenty years, and the other is that it is during these first six or seven years of life that a lifelong foundation for thinking is laid. Absorbing academic content can wait until first grade begins, but the early years are full of experiences that affect the way the mind works and whether it will be rich or poor in creative forces.

The First Three Years

One can say that the most fundamental steps in thinking are taken during the first three years of life when the child has traditionally been at home. During the first year, the child focuses on physical movement, gradually gaining control over his head, trunk, and limbs. Controlling the head, turning over, sitting upright, standing, and walking are the high points that every parent eagerly awaits. Around age one, once the child is able to walk erect, he leaves the horizontal realm and enters the vertical. A new perspective of the world enters the child's being.

During the second year, the child works actively on the acquisition of language. Words begin to come, at first usually nouns for naming objects. The child beings to group and sort the surrounding world through the naming process. Little Hannah, for example, was fascinated by the dog across the street. Her first word was "dog", and for some time "dog" meant any creature that moved, be it on four feet or on two. Gradually she learned that Mommy, Daddy, and other humans were not "dogs" but had their own names. Then she began to realise that not all four-footed creatures were called "dogs" as she distinguished them from cats, squirrels, and other animals. In Hannah, one could see that the development of language is more than the mere acquisition of words. It is a whole process of sorting out the world and relating to it.

Out of speech, the rudiments of thinking begin to emerge. The more able the child is to describe the world with words, the more the child begins to ponder the world and tries to understand it. Now comes the series of "Why?" questions, as the child seeks to understand the world. Why is the sky blue, the sun yellow? Answers about atmospheric conditions and burning gases have no real meaning to the young child, but answers about the qualities of nature and how they make us feel satisfy deeply. The child's mind understands that the blue sky is like a great blue blanket that stretches over us and makes us feel safe, whereas a yellow sun fills us with warmth. The three year olds challenge us to return to a place of imagination and wonder in our own thinking as we ponder their questions.

During the third year, as the child enters the realm of fantasy-filled thinking, several other major changes take place. At first glance, they do not seem related to thinking, but actually they are an integral part of it and show us much about the true nature of human thought. A most noticeable development is the use of the word "no" as the child enters the terrible twos. To the beleaguered parent, it seems as if a monster has entered the home, but all the child really wants to say is, "Step back and give me space. Something new is about to be born." What is new is an emerging sense of self, the beginning of a sense of "I". The word "I" is a most personal word that cannot be taught from without; it must arise from within. Prior to using this word, the child usually speaks of himself as "Johnny wants milk" or "Me wants milk". By now saying "I want milk," a new phase of self-awareness enters the child.

When this new sense of self enters, it often comes so strongly that one feels there is no room left in the child for a sense of "we". The child's social sense is pushed aside for the moment. It may seem that there is no one on the face of the earth quite so egotistical as a strong-willed three year old who has just discovered his or her own I. Consideration for others seems to disappear for a time, and only I-ness exists. Fortunately, the next stage of development brings forth an interest in the world, and the child begins to feel part of a larger social body again. The initial awareness of self is a necessary step for thinking because to think requires drawing into oneself. We do not stand in the centre of the marketplace to do our thinking. We retreat into the ivory tower of our own minds. Descartes (1960, 20) said, "I think, therefore I am", but the three year old seems more to say, "I am, therefore I think". The experience of "I am" and the experience of thinking go hand in hand.

There is one other major development in the child that coincides with the development of thinking around age three, namely, the birth of fantasy in the child. Often beginning around two and a half, the child's play becomes less reality based and more filled with fantasy. Banging on the pots and pans no longer suffices. Now the pot may become a house, and the spoon a person who lives in it. Offer a two year old — who is still engaged in sorting out reality — a bowl of sand and say that it is a birthday cake, and she is very apt to put it in her mouth. Offer it to a three year old, and she or he may look quizzically at you and ask, "It's make believe, right?" Offer it to a four year old, and he or she knows it is a play cake and proceeds to decorate it with sticks and leaves and calls her friends together for a birthday party. Fantasy, once born, allows children to play with the simplest objects and transform them into all that is needed for their play. Born around the same time as thinking, fantasy is a powerful partner to it. If fantasy is allowed to ripen side by side with thinking, these two faculties mature into creative thinking, a capacity to visualise not only how things are but also how they might be.

Regrettably, a great deal of modern education has misunderstood the importance of fantasy in the development of thinking. For the past twenty years or more, the cultivation of healthy fantasy in young children has been largely ignored in American early childhood centers. Emphasis instead has been placed on the development of rational, intellectual thought. From a Waldorf point of view, the absence of fantasy in the early years leads directly to the problems of stress, burnout, and the inability to think that now plagues so many American students. One of the great scientific minds of the twentieth century, Albert Einstein (in Stimpson 1988), understood the importance of fantasy as a critical part of modern human thought. "When I examine myself and my methods of thought," he said, "I come to the conclusion that the gift of fantasy has meant more to me than any talent for abstract, positive thinking".

The Kindergarten

If the child enters a mixed-age Waldorf kindergarten around age three and a half, then the "I" of the child is usually well established, and interest in life outside the self and home is beginning. The child enters the kindergarten at a time when his fantasy forces have been awakened and have begun to manifest in a lively way. His fantasy will go through several steps of development during the kindergarten years. At first, fantasy, young and fertile, bubbles up like the sweet porridge in the Grimm's fairy tale of that name. Like sweet porridge, it flows out everywhere. The child's fantasy is so full of activity and change that the three year old is more or less in perpetual motion. Gradually, the child becomes more focused in play, and the four year old can set up a play situation and remain with it for half an hour or more. The threes and fours, however, still have much in common in their play, for both are dependent on creating play situations out of what is at hand. They typically enter the kindergarten without an idea of what they want to play and wait for inspiration. This or that object captures their fancy, and their fantasy transforms it into what is needed. It is a great help to the growing fantasy if very simple natural objects are given as play materials. From these simple logs, stones, cloths, and other building materials, the child can create anything he needs, and his fantasy is not limited by defined objects. A fire engine that clearly looks like a fire engine is no use to a child who wants a space ship, or vice versa. But a handful of chairs, some cloths, and ropes can become any vehicle that the child desires.

A new stage of play consciousness begins with the five year olds, who often enter the kindergarten with an "idea" in mind. They do not wait for inspiration to arise from the objects at hand but start with an idea for play and then seek to create the objects that they need. They can easily stay with a play situation for an hour or longer and may play out the same idea for days on end. With the six year olds, this process goes one step further. They have an idea but often need few materials, if any, to carry out their idea. They will go through a period of time during which they take great pains to build a house or vehicle but take few props inside with them. Instead they "talk out" their play, expressing all the steps in play through conversation. That which previously took place outwardly with objects and busy limbs now takes place inwardly as imagination is born.

This change from fantasy play to imaginative play was beautifully described to me by Bronja Zahlingen, a well-known Waldorf kindergarten teacher from Vienna. As a child, she loved to play with small objects on a deep window seat in her bedroom. She would create a scene with little dolls and houses and play with them for long periods of time. She remembers that one day, when she was about six years old, she set up a scene as usual but then closed her eyes and played "inside". Imagination had been born, and she was able to participate in her play in a new way.

The development of imagination is an essential step in thinking, but where the development of fantasy has been curtailed, the development of imagination also suffers. Without imagination, one cannot picture an event in history, a verbal problem in mathematics, or the characters of a book. To approach academic subjects without imagination is a dull affair at best, and it is not surprising that children who are being educated without benefit of imagination at the elementary level find learning so uninteresting. Their newborn imagination is not being fed and nourished. Those who have been asked to master academics at the kindergarten level may suffer an even deeper problem, for in them imagination may be aborted before being born. There are indications that children who learn to read before age six or seven lose their early advantages, for they lose interest in reading and may eventually suffer burnout. This is not surprising when one thinks of how dull reading and learning are without benefit of imagination to bring them alive. In contrast, in my experience, the children who are the best players in the kindergarten and have the most active fantasy tend to become the most imaginative elementary pupils with the greatest interest in reading. They also tend to be the best-adjusted emotionally, both as children and even as adolescents and adults.

The relationship between success in fantasy play during the kindergarten years and later gains in mental development, as well as in social and emotional development, has been explored extensively by Sara Smilansky (1990) and others. They found that children who scored highest in what they called socio-dramatic play also showed the greatest gains in a number of cognitive areas such as higher intellectual competence, longer attention span, and more innovation and imaginativeness. The good players also showed more empathy towards others, less aggression, and in general more social and emotional adjustment. In addition, children who played well showed better ability to take on the perspective of others and showed fewer signs of fear, sadness, and fatigue. Smilansky's findings also point to simple, open-ended play materials as contributing more towards these developing materials. Her work is a strong confirmation of the relationship between fantasy play in young children and the development of capacities for strong thinking and a healthy emotional life (Smilansky 1990, 18-42).

Grades One to Eight

Between the approximate years of seven and fourteen, the intense physical activity of early childhood gives way to the feeling life of the child. Learning through imitation diminishes, and the child turns to the teacher in a new way, looking to her or him as a loving authority who knows the world. The pre-school child feels, "I can do whatever you can do through imitation." The elementary child feels, "There is so much I do not know, but you are my teacher and you know and will teach me." The path to knowledge for the school child is through the relationship with the teacher as a loving authority.

The Waldorf class teacher is faced with a number of challenges in working with the child. The curriculum is particularly rich and diverse, and the teacher is expected to offer creative presentations on a vast array of subjects over an eight-year period. The intellectual challenge to the teachers is enormous. Their own thinking is constantly stimulated, as well as their own creativity and love of learning. Moreover, they have to find the living relationship that they form with their class over the eight-year period. Relationships with the children and their families are worked on and deepened over these years, and the children benefit tremendously from the continuity of relationship. At the same time, they learn to relate to a variety of teachers, for they have speciality classes in subjects as varied as foreign languages, arts, handwork, gymnastics, and gardening.

Another aspect new to the school child is the freeing of the memory forces. Pre-school children often amaze us with the details that they remember of past events, but they can rarely call up memory at will. Rather, something is needed — a sound, smell, or sight — to trigger their memory, which then flows forth in abundance. By contrast, the elementary school children are able to go into their minds and find the memory that they seek, an essential quality needed for mastering academic subjects.

An additional change in the elementary children is that they are very interested in rules. One sees this in play, where games with rules now predominate over the creative fantasy play of the younger child. In learning, too, the child is ready to be guided by rules. The rules of mathematics and of writing make sense to the elementary child in a way that they cannot make sense to the younger child, for whom rules still have little inner meaning.

There are many other aspects of consciousness that awaken in the school child. Many are related to the maturation of the rhythmic system, for heart and lungs now settle into a regular rhythm, whereas in the younger child they are still quite irregular. With the development of the rhythmic system comes the love of rhythmic games such as jumping rope with verses, rhythmic hand clapping, and throwing balls to the accompaniment of long verses. Moving in a rhythmic way (for example, in counting and recitation) speaks deeply to the school child.

As the rhythmic system develops, the feeling life of the child comes more and more to the fore. Education can be cool and intellectual and bypass the feelings, or it can stir them deeply. The teacher approaches the curriculum in artistic ways, bringing to life a wide range of subjects. The love that the children develop in these years for the subjects that they study ripens into a deeper quest for knowledge in adolescence and beyond. One of the tasks of the Waldorf elementary teacher is to present the curriculum and feelings of the students, creating a context in which they can experience sympathy and antipathy, joy and sorrow, anger and tranquillity, and much more. Through mythologies, great stories, and stirring biographies, the children's own moral impulses are awakened, and an idealism begins to grow in them that will flower in adolescence.

High School

Around age fourteen, the more formed cognitive and intellectual thinking life of the teenager begins to develop strongly. Now the student works with teachers who are specialists in their fields. They guide the student through the phase of critical thinking so characteristic of the young teenager and help the older adolescent develop independent judgment. In the Waldorf high school, students are taught to observe and reflect so that they may arrive at their own conclusions about life. They are encouraged to examine problems from many points of view, so that their thinking can be well rounded rather than narrow. From deep within the adolescent, there awakens a quest for truth, and this pursuit of truth takes them on journeys as profound as those of King Arthur's knights seeking the Holy Grail. Indeed, an idealism enters their being at this time not unlike that found in the Grail seekers of old. The Waldorf high school teacher recognises that profound questions are stirring in the students, such as "Who am I? What am I doing here? What is it I am seeking in life?" The academic subjects, both in the humanities and in the sciences, open doors to those deeper answers that students are seeking at this age.

High school students experience so many changes in the physical body, emotional life, and mental realms that it is very easy for them to become unbalanced in their development. Many teenagers devote themselves so fully to the cultivation of social life that they have little energy left for the development of thinking. Others turn their energies so avidly toward sports that the development of thinking again suffers. Whereas a balanced interest in social life and sports aids thinking, an excessive interest in them diverts energy from thought. There are no foolproof ways for guiding young people through adolescence, but there is a much greater chance that their minds will be able to blossom in a well-balanced manner if their physical nature has had a healthy chance to develop in early childhood and if their emotional life has had the opportunity to deepen during the elementary school years.

Thinking in Adulthood

All that has taken place in the first two decades lays a foundation for the coming of age at twenty-one, when young persons experience a more profound birth of the "I" or individuality than that which took place at age three. Now they are ready to take on much more inner responsibility for their life's direction. Their "I" works through their thinking, feeling, and willing, and where these aspects of the self have been allowed to develop in a healthy and harmonious way, the "I" has a strong, clear instrument for its future use. If the instrument is damaged, then young adults will have to work extra hard to bring about a healing so that the individuality can sound forth in a clear and wholesome way.

If the mind is fertile and well related to the feelings and the will activity, then there are tremendous possibilities for growth and development throughout a whole life. Our self-education may then lead us into the new realms of thinking spoken of by Rudolf Steiner. He described the modern human being as standing on a threshold. New capacities for higher forms of thinking can now be developed that were not possible before. In the opening sentence to his book, *Knowledge of the Higher Worlds and Its Attainment* (1975), he writes, "There slumber in every human being faculties by means of which he can acquire for himself a knowledge of higher worlds." The challenge for the modern human being is to awaken these faculties.

This awakening is not an easy process, but Steiner gives exercises and indications for helping to bring it about in a healthy manner. The path is made easier if the faculties of thinking have been allowed to mature in such a way that fantasy and imagination ripen in their own time, and independent thinking filled with idealism grows in the adolescent. All of this, when coupled with a sense of wonder, opens doors to new ways of thinking. A renewal in thinking becomes possible and, through it, a renewal of all other spheres of life.

REFERENCES

Der Spiegel. 14 December 1981.

Descartes, R. 1966. Discourse on methods. In *Essential Works of Descartes.* Trans. L. Bair. New York: Bantam Books.

Eickelberg, W. 1991. In *The Results of Waldorf Education* (brochure). Kimberton, Penn.: Kimberton Waldorf School.

Healy, J.M. 1990. *Endangered Minds.* New York: Simon and Schuster.

Shipman, J. 1991. *The Results of Waldorf Education* (brochure). Kimberton, Penn.: Kimberton Waldorf School.

Smilansky, S. 1990. Sociodramatic play: Its relevance to behaviour and achievement in school. In *Children's Play and Learning*, ed. Edgar Klugman and Sara Smilansky. New York: Teachers College Press.

Steiner, R. published 1975: *Knowledge of the Higher Worlds and its Attainment.* Hudson, N.Y.: Anthroposophic Press.

Steiner, R. published 1979. *The World of the Senses and the World of the Spirit.* N. Vancouver, Can.: Steiner Books, Inc.

Stimpson, J., 1988. *Contemporary Quotations.* New York: Houghton-Mifflin.

Thesaurus of ERIC descriptors. J.E. Houston, ed. 1990. Phoenix, Ariz.: Oryx Press.

7

THE RESULTS OF WALDORF EDUCATION

What, really, are the results of Waldorf (Rudolf Steiner) education? One may feel that the brochures make Waldorf look excellent, and that the goal of "Education Towards Freedom" is very sound. One may be impressed by the enthusiasm and commitment of teachers in a Steiner school, and admire both the academic and artistic work of the students. But it is good to hear from people outside the Waldorf movement, who have worked together with — or in some other way have had experience of — Waldorf graduates, and who have an objective professional basis for judging whether this form of education really accomplishes its goals. The following three short articles, coming from California, New York, and Europe respectively, offer just this kind of professional and objective evaluation.

Results In The Waldorf Grade School

James Shipman

History Department, Marin Academy, San Rafael, California.

Explanatory Note: The Marin Waldorf School ends at Eighth Grade. A number of its graduates have gone on to the Marin Academy — not a Waldorf School — for their secondary education.

What I like about the Waldorf School is, quite simply, its graduates. As a high school teacher at Marin Academy, I have seen a number of the students who come from your program, and I can say that in all cases they have been remarkable, bright, energetic and involved.

One of my duties is to teach World Civilisations to incoming ninth graders, so I tend to be one of the first people who encounter a Waldorf graduate. My course is not like the standard History of Western Civilisation course, but rather requires the student to investigate the deeper aspects of the world's cultures. For example, we are not so much interested in the chronology of Chinese emperors and the dynasties to which they belonged; instead we want to explore and understand the principles of Taoism and Confucianism and how these underlying philosophies helped to shape the Chinese culture. We aren't so much interested in memorising names and dates as we are in understanding what motivates people, and why they make the choices they do.

I find the Marin Waldorf graduates to be entirely willing to undertake this sort of investigation. They are eager to learn. They do not complain when I assign, for example, a passage from the Bhagavad Gita and then ask them what they think. Indeed, that is what I find most remarkable about Waldorf kids: they have been taught to think; thinking is an "okay" activity for them to engage in. I think they intrinsically understand the difference between thinking about an issue and merely memorising "the right answer" for the test.

Waldorf students are not simply bookworms, however. In fact one could find Waldorf kids completely involved in the theatre, the arts, music and sports here at Marin Academy. What I see here is an integration of the faculties — mental, emotional, physical and spiritual — which, when coupled with the overtones of personality, unite to form unique individuals. Marin Waldorf students to me are interesting people. They can converse intelligently on almost any issue, because they have been taught to examine. They can be enormously sympathetic to almost anyone's plight because they have been taught to tolerate. They can gracefully dance or score a goal because they have been taught to move. They can circulate among the various groups on campus and engage in a variety of activities because they have been taught to harmonise.

We used to use the word "holistic" or "whole person" to describe the kind of person I have outlined above. Whatever the term used, it is apparent to me that the Marin Waldorf School consciously turns out calm, centred and confident students. For my part, I deeply appreciate the school's efforts, because based on their work, I get to enjoy those students who come to Marin Academy. It is with humility that I note that Waldorf students allow me and my colleagues to influence them. It is as if somewhere in their early years of schooling they somehow got the idea that learning is a lifelong enterprise.

The Waldorf Graduate: A Personal Reflection

Dr Warren E Eickelberg

Professor of Biology. Director: Pre-Medical Curriculum, Adelphi University, Garden City, New York.

Explanatory Note: Most, though perhaps not all of the students referred to here as "Waldorf graduates" had their high school years in a Steiner school.

The 1986-7 academic year marked my thirty-fourth year of teaching at Adelphi University. When I began, no biologist knew what a gene was and now we manufacture them. When I entered teaching, there were but a dozen antibiotics, and now they number in the thousands. Thirty-four years ago many of the biological sub-disciplines did not even exist and much of what we taught then would now be incorrect. The minds of men and women have opened for us new vistas to view; the hands of men and women have given us new technology, but the souls of men and women remain the same, always searching for the answers as to who we are, why we are here, and what our destiny is.

As there have been changes in academic content and technology, so the typical undergraduate student has changed. I lived with and experienced the job-oriented World War II veteran. I remember well the recall to active duty of many for the "peace action" in Korea. I sat through the "teach-ins" and the campus strikes of the Vietnam era. I lived through the revealing anatomy of the miniskirt, the drabness of the dark blue jean phase, the demands by the students to develop their own curricula, the re-orientation of learning by professors and administrators, the establishment of obviously immoral sex mores, the decline in admission standards, and the unique and possibly devastating effect that the medium of television has had on young people. Without any doubt, my past three decades have been marked by change, change and ever more change.

Throughout this dynamism of activity where values were under attack and standards of behaviour were challenged, from time to time there would be a unique stabilising influence in my classes: a Waldorf School graduate. And they were different from the others. Without exception they were, at the same time, caring people, creative students, individuals of identifiable values, and students who, when they spoke, made a difference.

Let me share with the reader some of these features so that you too might see the difference. Almost without exception, every Waldorf School graduate showed concern for the embalmed animals we use for dissection in Comparative Anatomy. I was always asked if the animal died painlessly, and they further questioned as to how. The Waldorf School graduates of the fifties, and of today, still show a unique reverence for life, and they regard an experimental animal, whether dead or alive, in a special way ... not just another reagent or piece of equipment to use in a laboratory exercise. Whereas most students are surprised to see the giant liver of a shark, it is always the Waldorf School graduate who sees this massive organ filled with oils as the result of a unique plan to give an animal buoyancy.

When describing geologic time, I have often told the true story of a man whose calculator could record the number 9.9×10^{99}. He discovered that even the estimated number of atoms in the universe or the volume of our known universe in cubic millimetres could not begin to approach this order of magnitude. It was a Waldorf student who found an article suggesting that the chances of two human beings, other than identical twins, being genetically alike would approach one out of 1×10^{6270}, and thus concluded that indeed each person is a unique and specially created individual.

We know the atoms in every cell of every living being are found in the stars and the intergalactic gases and that we all make up a Community of Matter. As we in science view the universe from its creation to its predicted end, man may seem, astronomically speaking, rather insignificant, but any Waldorf School graduate will remind each of us that Man is still the only astronomer.

Once, when I was discussing the decreasing gene frequencies of Blood type B from Siberia through western Europe, it was a Waldorf student who related this fact to the invasions by Genghis Khan and Tamerlane. It has been said that historians see civilisation as a stream though history, and the stream is often filled with blood, loud shouts, killing, and discoveries. Somehow it is the Waldorf School graduate who sees the stream, but also focuses on the banks where there are people who love, raise children, build homes, write poetry, worship, and carve statues.

Waldorf School graduates see behind the facts that often must be repeated or explained on examination. They are keenly interested in the macrocosm of the universe and microcosm of the cell's ultrastructure, but they know that Chemistry, Biology, and Physics can't tell them much about the nature of love. They see, in embryology, a foetus developing a compound called prostaglandin enhancing the mother's response to oxytocin so that labour can begin, and they see this as a reflection of a guided universe. I feel certain that all Waldorf School graduates believe in the orderliness of our universe, and they believe the human mind can discern this order and appreciate its beauty.

Beautiful Souls Or Initiative Takers?

This article was published in Der Spiegel, *a German weekly news magazine, somewhat analogous to the American magazines* Time *and* Newsweek; *in 1981.*

Waldorf Schools, generally reputed to produce "beautiful souls" weakened for the tasks of real life, actually do quite the opposite, say results of a study which could even correct the evaluation of Germany's Gesamtschulen (twelve-year schools which include both those students preparing for college and others as well). During the current school year (1981 — *Editors*) some 32 000 students were being educated outside the state school system in 72 Free Waldorf Schools, according to the pedagogical concepts of the founder of the school movement, Dr Rudolf Steiner. They attended a new type of school which, according to the aims of their founder, aspires to transmit not only knowledge and ability but also content helpful for life and a perspective on life's purposes. Their school day does not follow the 45-minute beat of strict timetables, but runs according to the rhythm of "blocks" and, during the first eight years, with strong artistic emphasis. Their career is not accompanied, year after year, by reports, marks and promotions, but is free of selection and pressures of grading — a tempting perspective surely, but for many parents hardly a realistic one or an adequate preparation for the battles of life. This view is now being shaken by a scientific study of "The Educational Background of Former Waldorf Students" — the first empirical research of the Waldorf movement.

Three independent scientists, paid by the Bonn Department of Education, interviewed 1460 former Waldorf students born in the years of 1946 and '47 and came to a prevailingly positive result in favour of the Waldorf Schools. Their students have achieved, so the examiners have discovered, "an educational plateau well above average."

The results appear to be formulated conservatively, for it is just this achievement of the Waldorf schools that holds surprises for the educational policy-makers. Twenty-two percent of the students polled passed the Abitur university entrance examination at their own Waldorf school — even back in the years 1966 and '67, almost three times more than in the state schools. Moreover, 40 percent of those polled, who had "never attended any other school than a Waldorf School" from grade 1 through 13, passed the Abitur. These statistics appear even more significant when the conditions under which the exams were taken are considered — for instance the fact that "the Abitur does not lie within the interests of Rudolf Steiner's pedagogy" as stated by Stefan Leber, Board member of the Association of Waldorf Schools.

Practically speaking, this means that the students are taught according to

Waldorf guidelines during their 12 years at school and are not specially prepared for the diploma examination. Only in the voluntary 13th year is the curriculum oriented towards the requirements of the state schools and the Abitur. On top of this, the exam itself was "an altogether unfamiliar Abitur given under strictest conditions: all tests came from outside the school; the exam was monitored by a state team of examiners." Proponents of the conventional school system must be irritated by such results because after all the Waldorf School is a Gesamtschule (see definition in first paragraph) of the purest type. Nevertheless it is now proven, says Bernhard Vier, who headed the research team, that "among the students who were taught for 12 years on a non-selective basis, an even higher percentage are able to pass the Abitur." All this, says the educator, "the academicians have never wanted to believe possible."

The Waldorf students showed a preference for occupations in the educational and social fields (20 percent), in the medical (12 percent), and in the artistic/linguistic field (12 percent); legal and technical professions were "under-represented". The graduates obviously took their incentives for professional choice from the Waldorf values. Success, prestige, recognition and career potential, and income played at best a subordinate role. As "personally especially important" in making their decision, the graduates named above all their own inclinations and abilities, independence and interests; then followed social and altruistic aspects.

8

THE ARTS IN EDUCATION: A BASIS FOR COGNITIVE DEVELOPMENT?

Stanford Maher

Again and again I am struck by the enormous disparity between what we require children to learn at school, and the evidence of what is needed in our daily lives. Driving in my car I have a number of radio stations at my fingertips which offer everything from classical to popular music. At home in my lounge, the television tempts me with one programme after another, either fiction stories or documentaries about people and their activities. If I opt for entertainment the chances are good I will attend a musical concert or see a film, play or ballet — more music, more stories in one form or another.

Why, then, is it that one could walk into most primary schools and find none of these activities taking place except as specialist subjects? Conducting a teacher enrichment programme in Cape Town, I asked the participants, all trained and experienced teachers, to what extent they used stories in their classrooms. The reply from one teacher was: "We were told at training college about the value of using stories, but the pressure to get through the syllabus is so great there isn't time to continue with stories after the first school year."

Without stories to stimulate the imagination so that learning can take place in an imaginative way, the classroom experience for many children is no more than the learning and memorising of facts. In most countries, budgets for the arts in education have been cut to a bare minimum. This is in line with the current survivalist mode of thought that believes nations can compete only if they develop a cutting edge in science and technology. Art in its various forms is seen as suitable only for relaxation — and let's face it, these days who can afford to relax? Throughout the world children are being relentlessly trained to compete on a global scale. This begs several questions, one them being the consequences of "educating" children without an artistic component being involved.

In Steiner education the arts are not taught as separate activities in the primary school, but are integrated into the general work of the classroom as enlivening teaching tools: drama, drawing, music, modelling, movement, painting and speech. The overall teaching method in these schools is intended to be artistic, through the teacher's work with the children. The basic task of the teacher, which is understanding individual children's learning needs and difficulties and finding the appropriate teaching response, hour by hour, is seen as an ongoing artistic occupation.

It is central to Steiner teaching methodology that while some of the work in the classroom is intellectual in nature, many concepts can be experienced only by learning on a different level, and this is where the arts come in. A child in the first grade has limited verbal skills and may not be able to read or write. By listening to stories containing images and words related to the learning concepts, she can gain her own understanding, in a way appropriate to her age, of the work the teacher wishes her to do. Through drawing and painting, she can express her understanding of these concepts. At the same time, she will gain practical skills in, and knowledge of, colour, form and perspective. By taking part in movement, she will experience physically with her body what can be transferred onto paper as letters, numbers and drawn shapes, as well as an understanding of the underlying concepts involved. If the work also contains daily recitation of poems and some simple classroom drama (as a learning experience, not for public performance) her education will be a rich one. She will be developing skills and capacities which cannot be acquired intellectually, any more than reading books could qualify one as a pilot of a jetliner. It is activity-based practical experience that is involved here. No amount of science or technology can give these very different skills and experiences, so an education which leaves them out of the curriculum is promoting a one-sidedness that can have definite consequences.

In South Africa the value of artistic methods in assisting the development of children, whether in or out of school, is particularly relevant. Many communities have been denied the expression that only a healthy involvement in the arts can give. This is tragic, because the humanising effect of an artistic education could significantly reduce the potential for violence among school pupils in disadvantaged, sometimes gang-ridden communities. It could also help to heal the effects of violence which has already occurred.

In fact, the information processing, fact-memorising approach so common in the South African black education system, has fed the potential for violence. It has done so because a purely intellectual education is specifically designed to stimulate and awaken the pupil's intellect. A consequence of this is that he will experience very sharply the frustrations of his life. If this process is untouched by the civilising and humanising influence of art, no healthy outlet is provided to balance these frustrations.

The arts should be seen not as soft subjects, but as important shaping forces in the learning process. The whole basis of civilised society throughout the world rests to a large extent on the transmission of culture through music, drama, literature, fine art, etc. In South African society many children have been brutalised by events arising out of, and fed by, ideological interests. What is now needed much more than refinements of the intellectual aspect of education, is a massive injection of the humanising values which come only through the integration of an artistic approach to teaching into school curricula, free of any ideological motive.

Because the arts transmit cultural and human values they have the potential to heal children traumatised by the many stresses in their daily lives. Our education system itself produces many such stresses. Adults know how irritable they can become when forced to sit through meetings in which one has to listen to others' ideas without a chance to respond or actively participate. Children in the state school system are required to listen on a daily basis to one teacher after another without the opportunity to move, act or respond to the concepts presented in any healthy way. And each of these teachers wants the children's undivided attention, no matter how tired they may be from the onslaught of the previous one. We know that pre-school children are primarily active beings. When they enter the first school class aged six years they are still these same active spirits. Sitting behind a desk and trying to grasp abstract concepts presented intellectually through books or on the chalkboard is death to their souls!

If the teacher has never been taught to draw or illustrate these concepts, if she has no idea how to lead the class in movement, if she cannot paint a picture, model an animal form in clay, plasticine or beeswax, lead her pupils in recitation or translate a suitable story into a simple classroom play (for her and her pupils' enjoyment only) how can she call herself a teacher? Without these skills she is forced to present concepts in their barest form, with no consideration for the fact that children learn differently from adults. The teacher then is simply not properly equipped to teach primary school children. Teachers themselves are beginning to recognise these realities. Many feel inadequate because they did not acquire these skills in their initial teacher training. It is clear that in future, a new kind of teacher training will be needed, one that provides these skills as a natural part of teacher education.

These basic techniques are necessary for them to appeal to the pictorial nature of the young child's thinking in all lessons, because they make the learning process more accessible to the child. In addition, because the child's thinking is naturally imaginative, this method of teaching promotes creative thinking. As children in the lower primary school depend heavily on non-literate skills such as drawing and modelling in clay or plasticine, in order to express their knowledge of the world, they are placed at a serious disadvantage if they do not have basic instruction in this area. The acquisition of artistic skills also leads directly to cognitive skills. Drawing, for instance, provides the opportunity to experience line and shape, colour, balance, perspective and the use of creative combinations. It lays a foundation for geometry and writing, among other things. Teachers all over the world encourage pupils to express their grasp of what has been taught through drawing, before they make the transition to writing, because it is one of the first ways in which the young child can express herself.

Rudolf Steiner noted that throughout the primary phase of schooling children operate out of a pictorial mode of thought which is qualitatively different from the adult's ability to think in the abstract. This means that the ability to communicate through pictures and images is all-important. Much effort in education is wasted because this simple and obvious fact has not been sufficiently acknowledged.

The fact that even adults with considerable experience in the business world find the pictorial method quicker to access, has been recognised by the corporate world. Companies which for years were only able to offer their staff computer software operating on the basis of intricate coded commands (in which the accuracy of the operating syntax was crucial), have now switched to the graphical user interface known as Windows, because it is easier for computer users of all ages to understand and operate. Pictures make things more accessible.

It is an indictment of the poverty-stricken state of modern education generally that in spite of all the evidence to the contrary, artistic work should be seen as a soft option, a break from "real" learning, and not as a shaping educational force in its own right, as valid as is mathematics. This has resulted in the paradox of our being able to appreciate the greatness of the culture of Ancient Greece, remembered today because of its artistic and cultural achievements, while at the same time dismissing the benefit of those activities as inappropriate for education in the twentieth century.

One reason for this appears to be that since the Renaissance, intellectual values have largely replaced artistic ones, and that in the twentieth century they have been placed in the service of technology. Our age is an expedient one and tends to value what is immediately measurable. The effect, however, is to throw the baby out with the bath water. The emphasis on acquiring knowledge through purely conceptual means ignores the evidence that this approach is inherently limited to *acquiring information*, rather than *developing capacities*. Intellectual work takes place at the level of ideas and concepts which are easily interchangeable. One fact can be replaced by another which is more convincing. There is a superficiality inherent in this which hints at the fact that deeper levels of the human being are being left untouched, namely the feelings and the will. The difficulty of attempting to change people's attitudes via an information approach is well known. Confronted with indisputable facts, people cling tenaciously to what has emotional meaning for them — their identity, their family group, their culture and their race. Information which is linked to feelings is much more effective in bringing about attitude change. This has significant implications for education. How do teachers help their pupils to develop tolerance for one another and to move beyond this to acquire feelings of community, brother and sisterhood?

Artistic learning activities offer a unique degree of freedom during the school years because they allow freedom to create, in comparison to the conformist approach followed in most other subjects. It follows therefore, that art can also promote creative thinking. This is proving essential in the Information Age in which we now live, because facts are rapidly replaced by new ones — in some instances before the learner has left primary school. It is obvious that in mathematics, pupils must necessarily arrive at the same answer. In painting, however, a pupil who arrived at the same "answer" as his neighbour would be demonstrating a lack of creativity. Different rules and methods of evaluation apply. However, both mathematics and art aim to develop in the pupil certain capacities which will prove beneficial in future life. Mathematics has been taught for centuries on the basis that it is not merely a set of computing skills, but that it teaches the ability to think in a logical manner. What then are the capacities which art can develop?

- Art allows experimentation. The combining of known elements allows the creation of something new.
- Art promotes communication for all children, but particularly for those whose verbal expression is inadequate.
- Art serves as an emotional release and therefore has great therapeutic value.
- It also heightens aesthetic awareness and sensitivity. The most disturbing development in education has been the emergence of young radicals who acknowledge no leaders. Their thinking is uncomfortably sharp, but their feeling for compromise through negotiation has not been developed.
- Art strengthens the self-concept and builds self-confidence . Self-confidence can be defined as a feeling of assurance in one's own judgement ability. In an educational system which "fails" so many pupils from disadvantaged backgrounds because they struggle with intellectual concepts, art can build self-trust and confidence on another level.
- Art enhances the ability to visualise.
- Art provides problem-solving and decision-making opportunities. The ability to see a mental picture which does not yet exist is central to artistic work. It is also essential for all innovation and experimental thinking.

How Art has been Used in Waldorf Schools as a Shaping Force in Education

In Steiner schools art is regarded as a shaping force in education. Just as the aim of mathematics is to teach children to think logically, so that of artistic work in any subject is to encourage creativity and lateral thinking through a search for *individual answers*. In a Rudolf Steiner school art permeates the entire curriculum. Teachers are required to prepare and present all subjects in an imaginative and artistic manner in order to make the learning material accessible and relevant to the child — in short, to make it human. Rudolf Steiner explained this by noting that information in the abstract is essentially alien to the child. He likened it to a cold meal which the teacher, out of her life experience is able to "warm up" for the pupil, in order to make the concepts accessible.

In addition, the lessons are structured to enable the pupils to engage with the learning material through their feelings and intellect, and to express their response artistically through a wide range of activities. Such a process naturally develops and harmonises the capacities of thinking, feeling and willing and acts as a preventative against a too one-sided development of any one of them.

To this should be added the fundamental premise adhered to in Steiner education, that the nature of the pupil's thinking is essentially pictorial rather than conceptual. To feed him concepts is therefore counter productive to the learning process, because little real understanding is achieved or retained.

The failure of educationalists to recognise this reality, more than any other factor, has contributed to the general loss of interest by pupils in their school work. The British educationalist Peter Abbs stated in a talk at Emerson College, Sussex, in 1978, that the abstract nature of modern education, fed by the information explosion, had already made the learning experience in schools so devoid of interest, that children had turned to the pop music culture in an effort to find interest and meaning in the world around them. The consequence, he says, is that schoolwork has become less relevant and meaningful in pupils' lives.

Rudolf Steiner stated that until shortly before puberty the child's consciousness normally has a pictorial rather than a conceptual character. He founded his elementary school methods on this basic recognition.

Comparing his methods with those of educators whose appeal was directed chiefly to the child's conceptual powers, Dr Steiner once asked, "I wonder what you would say if you were to see someone with a plate of fish before him carefully cutting away the flesh and eating the bones? You would certainly be afraid the bones might choke him and that in any case he would be unable to digest them. On another level, the level of the soul, exactly the same thing happens when we give the child dry, abstract ideas instead of living pictures, instead of something that engages the activity of his whole being."

These observations are particularly pertinent to the crisis in education in South Africa today. We have inherited a system which is failing pupils at both ends. In Sub A children are failing at such a rate that far fewer Sub B classes need to be provided for the following year. At the other end of the system, our school leavers are awarded Matriculation certificates which many employers judge to be worthless.

In both cases the reason is the same: the child in Sub A finds the learning material almost completely inaccessible because it is taught as intellectual concepts which she cannot access. The deprived cognitive background from which most pupils come makes the task of learning doubly difficult.

The teaching of concepts devoid of any imaginative content means that the pupil is forced to resort to learning parrot fashion. As his feelings are untouched by the learning process, he has to use a mechanical method in order to memorise for examinations material which has not been presented in a form which can be digested. The result is that our pupils have abilities only on paper, because their capacities are undeveloped.

Marjorie Spock argues that art forms the bridge between the child's experience of play and knowledge: "The child's whole being is called into play by an artistic education such as that conceived by Dr Steiner, for art speaks to the whole human being, not just to his thinking. Art fires the will and harnesses its strength through the objective discipline that each artistic medium imposes on the artist. Art profoundly engages the feelings. It develops that capacity for inward picturing out of which at a later age thought is born. Every art is centred, no matter how subtly, in the rhythmic element. During the child's elementary schooling when he is essentially a rhythmic being, art is therefore his natural province."

9

EDUCATION FOR TOLERANCE

John Coates

This article was originally written for and published by the UNESCO International Commission on Education for the 21st Century

How can Tolerance be Taught?

When one reflects on tolerance and education one quickly comes to the view that it is not like mathematics or history in that one may not regard it as a school subject and place it on the daily timetable. Rather it is closely related to morality, indeed even embedded in the mental health of the morally educated person, according to John Wilson[1]. Therefore the question "How can tolerance be taught?" immediately leads one into deep philosophical and pedagogical discussions requiring considerable time and space to do justice to it.

However, teachers are eminently practical people who often have little patience (tolerance!) for long, heavy philosophical argument. Even the little book by C.S. Lewis, *The Abolition of Man*, (which is essential reading for anyone interested in this area) requires more time and effort than many hard working teachers can afford to give. Therefore a few practical suggestions which flow from Waldorf Education will be given. In Waldorf Education "respect for the worth of every individual's abilities is fostered in a spirit of co-operation and tolerance. Emphasis is placed on the development of social and interactive skills" [2]. It is an educational approach which pre-eminently cultivates a favourable ground for the promotion of tolerance.

One of the basic pedagogical principles of this approach is that the developing child — especially during the years of 7 to 14 — grows most strongly in his feeling life. If these feelings and emotions are cultivated so that they respond appropriately to what is good, true and beautiful in their environment, then the power to act and behave appropriately in social life is built up within them. For example, in teaching about the voyages of discovery, the teacher can help his pupils to enter as vividly as possible into the topic under discussion — e.g. Magellan rounding Cape Horn.

Using a wide variety of methods like descriptive story-telling, classroom dramatisation, poems, choral speech work and creative writing, the teacher can help the children feel the terror experienced by the sailors as their little ship fought its way back and forth through the mountainous white seas expecting any minute that it would be ripped to pieces on the black, towering rocks or disintegrated by the howling winds. If the children can live into this experience as deeply as possible and feel the tremendous relief, almost disbelief, upon the ship reaching the ocean which the sailors called Pacific, then their feelings will be cultivated and refined and they themselves will be ennobled by the experience.

This may appear to be a long way from tolerance but the interest generated in this vicarious experience, this experiential re-living of an historical event helps to ennoble the growing child's soul. Later on these qualities may be called into action when as an adolescent he or she confronts injustice in one form or another. She is then enabled to enter more fully into the full circumstances of the situation or occasion and then after arriving at a balanced resolution have the resourcefulness to take appropriate action.

A group of Class 7 (Standard 5) pupils from the Waldorf School in Johannesburg was traveling through a small conservative town in the Northern Transvaal during the days of "grand apartheid". The class contained the first Zulu child to be admitted to the school (Waldorf schools were among the first schools in South Africa to enrol children of all races). The children merrily piled out of the bus and headed for the only shop in sight. Busily they started collecting their bottles of cold drinks and sweets for the remainder of the journey. One child, the black Zulu boy, was, however, singled out by the shopkeeper and told bluntly that he was not allowed to enter the shop which was reserved for whites. Some of his classmates, on witnessing this, went straight to their teacher and reported the incident. The teacher[3] listened to them and then asked them what they would like to do about it. The children with one voice expressed their indignation at the treatment of their classmate and decided to leave the shop without their intended purchases.

The message was spread quickly to the entire class and with a sense of conviction each child replaced their goods on the shelves, stormed out of the shop and piled into the bus. If their black friend could not be served, they refused to purchase. This was quite a decision for hungry and thirsty travel-weary youngsters to carry out, more especially as they were unsure of where else they could buy their goods.

Another basic method in Waldorf Education is to present all concepts initially to the young child in pictorial or living form. This is a skill which is quite foreign to most adults today, but well enshrined in the fables, myths and legends of all nations. The Statue of Liberty in New York harbour or the Fates in Greek mythology are good examples of this approach.

No doubt there are many ways to teach a young child how to tie a knot. One may say "Now you take one end in your right hand and the other in ..." or one may say "Now there were these two yellow snakes. One was making his way through the grass when he crossed over another ..." The young child will listen more intently to the snake story because it satisfies his imagination and then it leads naturally to the task behind the story. With the primary school child one of the ways to communicate successfully is through this ability to create pictures — not static photographic-like images but ones which move, live and vibrate. Oscar Wilde's *The Selfish Giant* is far more moving for children than many a lecture on selfishness. Even the four processes in basic arithmetic may be more intelligible when presented, for instance, as a king's four children, Adam, Minus, Sharem and Multiferus, each of whom had a special ability and a very definite temperament.

Indeed, perhaps selfishness is more basic than tolerance!

Tolerance appears as a natural quality of the younger child while intolerance appears to be bred by adults. Like all Waldorf schools in South Africa the local one to which I sent my children was non-racial, multi-cultural, and unstreamed. My youngest son, David, was a very slow developer and on entering the school, his speech was unintelligible even to his parents. However, as his class teacher felt he could work with him, he was accepted. One mother related to me that her son, Peter, told her that there was a very nice new boy in the class called David — who was learning to speak English!

A Waldorf teacher reported that his young son one day spoke vehemently about "Bloody blacks ..." His mother, shocked at this racialist outburst, reminded him about the black children in the class. "How about Sally, Pierre and Sipho?" "Oh, no" replied her son "they're my friends — they're not Blacks!" A good proof that racial differences become insignificant when friendship blooms.

As the same teacher pointed out, many of the images or models presented by the mass media today, such as Superman, Batman, Ninja Turtles, Hunk, to name but a few, are heroes without substance. The important question is, do these images address the inner moral fabric of the child? I once overheard a neighbour threatening his seven year old daughter with a visit by Hunk if she refused to do what she was told! Perhaps it is best to preserve children from these images.

It is possible, using fables taken from many lands to present animals as embodying the quirks of human behaviour. Through hearing and living with the fables at an early age (Class 2 in the Waldorf curriculum) the children learn how to overcome these tendencies. However, there is no intellectualisation of the content by the teacher, no mention of a moral or lesson to be learnt. Rather the fable is left to speak on its own to the child. The fable lies like a seed in the ground of the child's soul to grow in its own time.

Likewise fairy tales, stories of the saints, myths and legends, are given to the children. They are often worked into poems, stories, and class plays. In the case of the latter, many opportunities await the observant teacher who can cast a child in a role that demands the presentation of characteristics which he does not as yet possess. Indeed, there is the drama teacher who cast the most voluble teenager in the class as the silent soldier who had to remain highly attentive and reactive, but mute, in very dramatic scenes. A unique way to learn tolerance! Parents are often amazed at the transformation which this emphasis on classroom drama can generate.

One of the important qualities of any teacher, but especially a high school teacher, is humour — the ability to see the humorous side, even to be able to laugh at one's self. Even more important is the skill to defuse a potentially explosive situation. A colourful incident was related to me as an example.

A Class 11 (Standard 9) Science lesson was in full swing, when suddenly the door burst open and in barged a latecomer. There were no apologies for the lateness, but complete indifference. Indeed, his whole attire spoke eloquently for him. He was totally unsuitably dressed for school (smart casual was the requirement) with slashed jeans, torn, dirty shirt and uncombed hair. He therefore grabbed the immediate attention of the class in a highly confrontational manner. The teacher[4] could not ignore the situation and proceeded to reprimand him in the clearest possible terms. Before long the situation had deteriorated and a potentially explosive and rebellious pupil stood before an irate teacher. The previous day the teacher had confiscated a small Christmas cracker type plastic gun and as the climax of the argument approached, he produced this plastic gun and pretended to shoot the boy. Immediately everyone in class collapsed laughing and the tense situation was broken without either party losing face. The next day the pupil arrived on time — with top hat and tails, white shirt and bow tie! Humour can often win the day and bind a class together!

In order to cope with the restlessness and urge to test out their as yet unproven skills in the work situation, the Waldorf schools send their 16/17 year olds on what is called the Social Practical. This involves the pupils working for two weeks in organisations or institutions where people are less fortunate than themselves. This may entail work in a sheltered employment factory, a home for retarded children or a school for the deaf.

There is the example of a boy and a girl who chose to attend a Camphill Village, a protected environment for handicapped adults, some 100 km outside Cape Town. However, after a week there they were asked to leave because of their misbehaviour. They then moved to an institution also for retarded adults closer to their homes. The pupils were now amazed at the enormous difference between the institutions. At Camphill the villagers were given real community life where each one was dependent on the other — in fact a mini-town geared to a level where the inmates felt secure and able to prosper. The other institution looked after the inmates physically but provided no cultural or community responsibilities. It is only with a particular understanding of the human being that the possibility arises of opening up a cultural environment.

This may flow from an understanding that each human being has a particular destiny and that the child comes from the spiritual world and returns back to it. This one does in cycles and therefore one is less judgemental of a person because he/she is seen as passing through various stages.

This spiritual or divine aspect was highlighted by two African squatter camp teachers[5], who recently attended Novalis teacher training courses based on Waldorf educational principles.

Question: How has what you've experienced on this course helped you to be more tolerant?

Halbert: The first thing that came to me on the course was that the lecturers seemed to possess that which is the basis of African culture. This was the flavour of African tribal tradition that binds us together — distinctions disappear in an instant — we become one family. This is an intense feeling. It is a sense of touch which has to do with the divine world. Something changed within us. It is a spiritual touch which works with all other aspects and brings out a feeling of love and kindness.

Adolphus: I found the work very original and it brought us to the roots which have long been left by us or our elders. The tutors promoted an understanding among ourselves.

Halbert: Our relationships were improved. We became more open with the children. Before this we were not able to play with the children. Now we can play with them, enjoy the element of play or games. Another side was also introduced — art. Before we began these courses we were illiterate on that side. We knew nothing about the different colours etc. We began to understand ourselves, our strengths and weaknesses and out of ourselves have discovered a lot.

Adolphus: We have learned to accept ourselves as human. We are even able to make a mistake in front of the children.

Halbert: The morale and confidence in the school has been boosted so that our pupils are happier, more confident people.

The management and administration of a school helps to create an atmosphere which can be conducive or threatening to the promotion of tolerance. In the Waldorf approach a working collegiality exists among the teachers so that the schools are managed without the traditional role of a principal of head teacher. This involves considerable and constant working together of teachers in order that the interests of the whole school, its teachers, parents and pupils are carried in a personal and professional way by the entire staff. This kind of working together is not easy, but a continual growing in tolerance and in appreciation of the unique contribution of each staff member becomes a process that is highly valued.

Similarly, among the pupil body the traditional prefect structure is completely absent. Having witnessed three of my children pass through this non-authoritarian and non-hierarchical system of pupil management I see it as a powerful aid in the growth process of tolerance and individuality.

Tolerance therefore appears to be a quality which is cultivated through a wide variety of activities — stories, plays, poems, festivals, arts, crafts, games, dance — the list is endless. Indeed, it is promoted whenever people meet each other. In particular schools provide great opportunities for us to develop this important social skill. Strangely, too, as tolerance appears also to be a natural quality of very young children, maybe that is a good reason for us, adults, to go to school! we have an important lesson to learn (re-learn).

REFERENCES

1 John Wilson, *et al.* *Introduction to Moral Education*, Penguin 1967.
2 *Prospectus* Michael Oak Waldorf School, Cape Town, South Africa. Page 2.
3 Conversations with Mr S Maher of Novalis Institute, Cape Town.
4 Conversations with Mr E Fox of Constantia Waldorf School, Cape Town.
5 Conversations with Mr Halbert Mlindagwe and Mr A. April of Bongolethu Community School, Cape Town.

10

ENVIRONMENTAL EDUCATION IN WALDORF SCHOOLS

Andreas Suchantke

Introductory Note

Waldorf education attempts to work on the principle of matching the style and content of teaching to the pupils' stage of development. It recognises that children in the lower primary classes are very different from those in the classes above them, not only in their cognitive abilities but also in the way they experience their surroundings. The methods at this level must therefore be different from those used with children approaching or already in their teens. Matching method to age here means being able to do justice to the children's capacity for strong emotional involvement in what they are taught. Achieving this provides a solid basis for the more scientific and practical approach to the same subjects that comes later, for it has a powerful influence upon the child's subsequent ethical attitudes. Since the methods used in the lower primary classes have such far-reaching importance and are unique to Waldorf education, this whole area will be dealt with at some length in what follows. This in no way implies, however, that less weight is given to science education.

The Social Climate

It goes without saying that children are moulded to a large extent by the attitudes they meet at home. Only very few will have environmentally active parents. With regard to the environmental crisis most people are either indifferent or thick-skinned, or simply stick their head in the sand — they have no other way of coping with the daily horror reports.

Added to this, many children in the industrialised countries are caught up in a life-style which estranges them from nature. "Nature" is something you drive through, or "experience" in television films. The child's natural environment pales into insignificance beside the sensations pictures shown in such programmes.

All in all, therefore, the conditions for environmental education are not exactly favourable. One example, typical in its own way, may be used to illustrate this:

A young, inexperienced teacher had just taken on class one at a large urban Waldorf school in Germany, and found herself completely at a loss in the face of the chaotic unruliness of the children. To provide an outlet for the children's excess motor activity she had the idea of taking them on a walk every morning. Having embarked upon this course of action she was shocked to find "the hostile attitude many children had towards plants and small animals. It could only be described as a 'chase-trample-squash mentality'".

On the other hand, many young people (and children) are actively involved in conservation. In every community there are youth groups busy in the cause of nature — bird watching, looking after nesting-boxes, etc. The major conservation organisations draw in large numbers of young people, who take part in all sorts of activities with greet enthusiasm. Altogether, however, it is still only a minority which is motivated in this way.

Finding One's Bearings in the Field of Environmental Education

The question naturally following on from this is: what can, indeed, what must the school do in order to promote and nurture this attitude in a large proportion of children and young people? That the social climate for this is not easy is shown by the previous example. Since, however, this is a challenge of the times and also a great opportunity, all conceivable lines of approach to it should be undertaken.

Before pursuing this question from the point of view of Waldorf education we must briefly look at two differing approaches within the field of environmental protection. The difference between them is educationally of great significance, as will be shown.

- The *anthropocentric* approach is concerned with the quality of human life and attempts, by cleaning up technology, by making consumer products more environmentally friendly, by reducing exhaust emissions, finding alternative technologies, avoiding waste, introducing poison-free agriculture etc, to reduce environmental impact and thus make the human environment safer.

- The *ecocentric* approach is directed towards nature for its own sake: the protection of whales and other threatened forms of animal and plant life, or the preservation of precious ecosystems, etc. The question as to their possible usefulness for humans is not asked.

Both positions are perfectly justified and are not opposed, but rather mutually enhance each other. A purely anthropocentric approach will only ever be cosmetic, concerned with the curing of symptoms, because it is not focussed upon what keeps the life of nature (the soil, the forests etc.) healthy. Behind it lies the long-standing assumption that nature is an infinitely exploitable reservoir of resources, which must simply be used more intelligently in future. This assumption overlooks the fact that survival is only possible within a healthy biosphere, which can only remain so as long as man respects its own laws and requirements.

This latter attitude is inherent in the ecocentric approach. But ecocentricity is strong in another respect: It appeals to the idealism latent in many, if not most, young people. It opens up the possibility of committed action on behalf of something not just worthwhile, but disadvantaged, oppressed and exploited. Ecocentric action has a strong emotional appeal. People who put their all into fighting for a good cause in this field make a strong impression on the young. Not by chance are Greenpeace activists the modern heroes. In this we have an interesting parallel to developments that took place in the last century and the first half of this one. Social conscience, which developed in the struggle for the rights of slaves, serfs and the industrial proletariat, is today being extended beyond the human world towards nature. To encourage this development in every way possible must become the central task of education.

Here, unlike other subjects, we are not likely to have any difficulties in motivating the pupils. A mainly anthropocentric approach will not have such a ready audience, as has been shown very clearly by Langeheine and Lehmann (1986) They found that although this approach raised the level of knowledge it created little motivation towards environmental action. It was merely an informative exercise, devoid of any emotional involvement.

Meeting Nature

Let us begin by recalling the teacher whose young pupils behaved so aggressively and destructively towards animals and plants. In seeking for ways to improve the children's relationship to nature she began telling them stories about animals and plants. These were not little catalogues of scientific facts, but told, in an imaginative way, of such things as what a raindrop hanging on a leaf-tip sees, what the ant says to the snail when they meet. Gradually the children began to listen and to demand more stories. In time their behaviour outdoors also changed: a snail was carefully carried out of the way, so that it would not be walked on. Under the influence of the stories the children began to discover nature, the plants and animals. A positive relationship had arisen, and this was further developed. Friendly affection for nature developed and was extended and deepened over the years: a particular piece of woodland, through which a stream flowed, was repeatedly visited, seasonal observations were made and much more besides. "Soon it was our path, our stream, our tree and park, our squirrels and blackbirds. If the stream dried up in summer, the children were sad and perplexed ("where has our water gone?") and wanted nothing more than to give the stream bed back its water. This was soon joined by the inner urge to find the cause of the streams drying up — and in due course this was found." The observations led to the first awakenings of thinking, to the beginnings of a genuine research mentality.

Most important, however, is the fact that not until a loving attachment to plants and animals, to woodland and stream, has arisen, can a caring, protective relationship come about. If the emotional level is neglected no identification with the phenomena takes place. "Scientific" teaching that approaches things in a cognitive, rational way either too early or too exclusively prevents any emotional connection to the object arising, and is surely the least appropriate method for developing ethical responsibility.

The Affective Relation to Nature during the Early School Years

The method used by this teacher is a prime example of that generally used in Waldorf schools. It is based upon taking account of certain concrete facts of developmental psychology and using them in practice. Thus it is assumed that children of pre-school and primary school age experience reality in a different way to young people and adults. The resulting age specific teaching methodology is based upon principles which are broadly in tune with the discoveries of the school of Piaget, even though they were developed quite independently (e.g. Steiner 1919, 1921-22).

The experiential world of the child up to the age of 10 is not one of external objects, as is that of the adolescent or adult. Rather it is animistic — there are no mere "things", since everything is experienced as animate. The tree, the moon, the stone are all sensitive beings imbued with feelings like the child. And these beings are not in any way isolated phenomena, but stand in direct relation to the child. The moon follows the course of an evening walk because he wants to know where the child is going; (Piaget 1926). What we have is a picture of a unified, closed world of related beings, surrounding the child who stands in the middle. The child is still embedded in a world where everything has its proper place and is directed towards him or her. Alienation is still unknown. Of course, nowadays that is all overlaid to a greater or lesser extent by influences from the world of the media. That what we have here is a masking of the infant's true mode of experience, and not its destruction, is shown by the example with which we began. Such experiences can always be repeated, as long as the teacher manages to keep his or her head, and is truly committed.

Premature use of cognitive-abstract, "scientific" teaching methods, on the other hand, would only intensify the tendencies called forth by over-exposure to the electronic media; tendencies that would wrench the child too soon out of its empathic milieu. This separation takes place of itself in the course of the first years of school with the gradual awakening of the ability to form general concepts and to cope with operational and causal thinking. This development should not be artificially forced, rather it is much more important to let the prior "animistic" phase run its full course. If this is allowed to fade later rather than sooner, it will, when alienation finally sets in, provide a basic feeling of relatedness to the environment, to nature. This is the essential basis for the possibility of a new caring attitude to nature forming at the level of cognitive knowledge and action.

Teachers (not forgetting those in the kindergarten) of the primary classes will be dealing with natural phenomena in an appropriate way if they take into account a further faculty of this age-group. This is the ability to realise imaginative pictures inwardly. Stories, fairy tales etc are experienced with such living, moving, pictorial intensity that the child does not stand in a reflective relation to the contents of the story, but is completely involved. In this way these pictures are more intensely real for the child than is the world of external objects. The latter is experienced to the extent that it is permeated with soul.

Introducing children to nature, therefore, will not begin with any sort of demonstration involving actual animals and plants being brought into the classroom, but with story telling. These stories, invented or embellished by the teacher, should not be fantastic, but rather imaginative, and need not shy away from real situations. Thus what happens first is a broadening of the inner horizon. Then, in the second step, on walks and excursions, actual meetings with the relevant objects take place. Without anything being said the children discover ants, dewdrops etc, for themselves. They perceive them because they are already familiar with them "inwardly". Every encounter thus becomes a joyful re-discovery. And this goes also for children who are estranged from nature and overloaded with media influences, as were the ones in our opening example.

From Natural History to Natural Science

Nature study begins in earnest once a particular step in the process of separation from this feeling of oneness with the world has been taken. This first emancipatory step immediately strengthens the child's awareness of his or her own self in contrast to that of his or her own fellows. People and the world are now "other" than oneself. If plants, animals, stones, trees and the moon were originally experienced as animate, this now fades gradually into the next phase, in which only that which moves is animate, and finally, at the age we have now arrived at (age 10) only that which moves itself, i.e. man and animal, is experienced thus.

This separation and incipient alienation provides for the first time the basis for having any experience at all of something "other", and for realising its specific quality. Only now does objectivity become possible, while a keen interest in the world and in nature begins to make itself felt. Questions are asked as to the particular characteristics of this or that animal etc. Sensory perception also attains a new quality. The children begin to discover lots of things in the world around them; they develop into excellent observers of the natural (and human) environment — a concept which only now becomes fully justified.

This interest and these questions are an expression of the children's need to re-fashion their dissolving union with the beings around them on a new level, that of understanding and knowledge. This need must now be met in every way possible. Accordingly, in the first block of animal study in class four (age 10) the attempt is made to tease out the specific "motif" of each of the animals looked at. Most animals have a typical specialisation, i.e. a certain ability which is functionally very highly developed — for instance, the sense of sight in birds of prey (eagles), the mastery of limb activity in climbing rocks (ibex) or trees (squirrel), the process of digestion in ruminants. Out of each respective speciality can then be derived a connection to a specific place in the environment, a particular "niche". Both mutually enhance each other and they fit together like lock and key. The two aspects that apply to every living thing are thus covered: the characteristics typical of the species and the integration into the structure of the ecosystem in which the animal, or plant, lives.

And there is something more. The teacher's task is not simply to introduce the animal, but to describe its behaviour in such a lively way that the pupils are intensely involved. If, for instance, the bold agility of an ibex is being described from the point of view of an eagle, whose keen gaze nothing escapes, then the children experience anew their relationship to these living creatures. They experience — not consciously, of course, this is not directly referred to — "I too am eagle, ibex" etc. This often finds expression in a way which is very clear, even if the children are not consciously aware of it. If the description of the ibex and his incredible climbing abilities gets too dramatic they will start playing "ibex", and then the classroom turns into a rodeo. A melancholic child, by contrast, is likely to be more attracted to the shellfish. It hides its treasures (pearl, mother-of-pearl) deep inside under an unobtrusive shell; etc.

But is this environmental education? It is one facet of what goes on in Waldorf schools. We consider it a particularly important one. It is characterised by a continually renewed search for the bridges that join man to nature: in the young child at the affective level, at the cognitive level when natural history begins, leading gradually over into the scientific approach.

Again this is found in the teaching of ecology, which in many Waldorf schools (especially those in Scandinavia) takes up a lot of space in the various subjects of classes eight and nine (age 14-15). Thinking in ecological concepts trains the intelligence, as it involves complex interactions and relationships. Here a strong point of curricular emphasis is geography, which includes consideration of: the climatic and edaphic basis for the formation of the world vegetation zones, together with knowledge of their ecological peculiarities as a basis for their sensible, use; mistakes of the colonial period and modern intensive cultivation in comparison to the (disappearing) highly adapted methods of indigenous peoples; the significance of the oceans, the forests, questions of global and local conservation; anthropological aspects of ecology. In the area of biology, in addition to the basic principles of scientific ecology, worthy of special mention is: ecosystem development (genesis, succession, long-term change as a result of tectonic plate activity, etc). In evolutionary biology co-evolution is considered as well as the classical picture.

Just for the sake of completeness, the wide range of possibilities offered by chemistry may be mentioned; for instance, the carrying out of analyses of toxic substances, water, etc.

In the twelfth and uppermost class (age 18) a grand synthesis is attempted, the aim being "Gaia", in other words the earth grasped as a whole in its differentiation as well as in its evolution. This includes looking at the character and function of the different kingdom of nature; the ambivalent position of man with his facility both for destruction and for contributing creatively to the evolutionary process; the relationship between nature and culture, between biological and mental evolution.

The Social Aspect of Ecology

As previously stated, we are nowadays experiencing the extension of social awareness beyond human society towards nature. The effects of this are being felt from the field of conservation to the administration of justice. These tendencies are strongly supported by the results of modern scientific ecology. These have led to a decisive re-think of the received picture of evolution as driven exclusively by a "struggle for existence". Of particular importance in this connection is the insight that any organism is embedded in its ecological surroundings in a two-fold way. On the one hand it contributes to the preservation of its species by reproduction, while on the other hand it plays a specific part in the preservation of the ecosystem to which it belongs. Plants as "producers" facilitate the existence of the animal kingdom and of man. Through the pressure of their hunting predators control prey populations, thus keeping them at a level which the ecosystem can tolerate, while at the same time preventing them from overbreeding and consequently exceeding the capacity of the food supply. The activities of earthworms play a decisive role in the life of the soil and in plant growth; through their decomposing activities bacteria and fungi manage the flow of nutrients back into the soil where they then become available for plant growth.

A similar dual relationship exists in human society. On the one hand, everyone has a right to satisfaction of the basic needs of life and to the fulfilment of certain personal aims. At the same time, each person, through the exercise of his or her profession, makes some contribution to the general well-being.

More important than this comparison, however, is the fact that in nature there are no "one way streets", in the sense that something is taken and nothing given back. To realise this as a basic fact of experience — as experience, let me repeat, and not as indoctrination — quite naturally provokes the question as to whether the exploitative attitude man has so far had towards nature, without a thought of contributing something towards her continued existence, is justified. And if nature is "bleeding to death" at our hands, is this not a consequence of this very same attitude, and the fact that we have still to make the necessary contribution to her healthy survival?

If this is to become a part of experience then we must at this point step into the realm of practical activity.

Fieldwork

The incorporation of fieldwork — the active care of nature — into various subject areas is necessary in order from the outset to avoid the mistaken attitude previously mentioned; this being that the pupils might well attain to well-founded knowledge, and perhaps even to the development of a sound ethical attitude, yet still refrain from responsible action. A leading figure of the contemporary scene is the person who is well-informed but incapable of action. He is ultimately the reason why so little happens to stave off the threatening ecological catastrophe. The primary aim of education, of whatever kind, must therefore be to lead pupils to genuine maturity which enables them, on their own initiative, to take hold of what they have experienced and felt to be right and put it into practice.

The most suitable way of giving pupils a first field experience of taking care of the natural environment is to place them in a traditional cultivated landscape as diverse and intact as possible. This has been shaped by man, but at the same time provides habitats for a rich diversity of indigenous, undomesticated plants and animals (Pott 1988, Suchantke 1993). In Waldorf schools gardening as a subject begins in the kindergarten, albeit entirely at the level of following what the teacher does. In this way the children experience sowing, germinating, blossoming and ripening. They learn also about what bees and earthworms do.

A block on farming in class three (age 9) takes up the threads of this motif once more, with the difference that now the pupils are the ones who do the work. A piece of land is ploughed, harrowed and then sown with corn. Its growth is then observed. Then later it is harvested, threshed, the grain ground into flour and finally made into bread. Where possible this activity will take place once a week for a whole or half a day on a suitable local farm. Here the children will have the chance to see all the other things that go on, how the animals are handled etc. In all this the children will have experienced for themselves that only through intensively tending the crop is the right to harvest it earned, and that the caring attention involved must take account of the plants' and animals' living requirements.

But something else of no lesser significance is involved in this little exercise, for through it children can experience the fact that man is perfectly capable of working together with nature to the mutual benefit of both. The widely held opinion that man is in principle only capable of acting destructively towards nature is demonstrably false and stems from "biology's acultural image of man" (Gropengiesser and Kattmann 1991). In all cultures there have been periods of constructive partnership with nature, which did not just benefit man, but also gave nature manifold evolutionary stimulation (Abel 1978, Suchantke 1993).

These well-supported facts can form part of the content of a range of subjects — geography, history, biology. This of course does not in any way imply a playing down of the gross errors being committed to-day, but the latter do appear in a different light when viewed in such a context. Instead of being left with a thoroughly demoralising, one-sided view of man as "disturbance" of nature, we are encouraged to consider other possibilities.

That which is simply a little episode in class three, i,e. the main-lesson block on farming, becomes a constant feature of the timetable of the middle school (classes 6-9/10) as the subject gardening, which culminates in a two-week field practical. This is the agricultural practical in class 9: which may be followed by one in forestry in class 11.

Rudolf Steiner justified the introduction of gardening as a subject in the following terms: "People who have had this subject in school will be able to decide whether an agricultural method or treatment is right or wrong not because they have learnt about it, but out of the accuracy of their feelings. This subject is also a moral training. Its true effects will only become apparent in the social behaviour of the adult". These words anticipate the crisis of modern agriculture, while at the same time suggesting a way of solving it. Agriculture has long been the concern of society at large and the direction it takes is ultimately determined by consumer behaviour. But all potential influence from this quarter is undermined by indifference, and by ignorance of what farming is about. This situation would change radically the moment gardening or agricultural practicals were made a part of general schooling. The school subject envisaged in the quotation is not intended to produce future gardeners, but to school "accuracy of feeling". Whoever has devoted himself for a certain length of time to a particular activity develops a "feel" for it, that tells him whether this or that method is appropriate. It will also (if it has been done properly) acquaint him with its typical problems, and it is in coming to terms with these that the previously mentioned "moral training" takes place.

The Teacher's Contribution: Initiative and Commitment

So far we have been concerned mainly with the curricular dimension, with everything that has its established place in the Waldorf curriculum. As the example of the class one teacher we began with shows, however, none of this is of much use unless it is brought to life by the teacher's own initiative and imagination.

The Waldorf curriculum does not simply leave the teacher free to make something individual of the usually very generally described subject areas, but represents a direct challenge to use this freedom. The teacher carries the primary responsibility for his pupils. Only he has the knowledge of their individual capabilities and stage of development that can inform the decision as to how to proceed in terms of method and content. No wonder then that it is mostly independent individuals with high pedagogical motivation who decide to become Waldorf teachers.

The consequence of this is that in the realm of environmental education, just as in other subject areas, we are confronted with an almost impenetrable diversity of activities. Thus it is only possible to name a few representative examples, which must stand in for the hosts of others left out of account.

In the lower and middle school, camping expeditions with a particular theme are a regular feature of the year (especially in Swiss and Norwegian schools). They focus on plants, water, geology, etc, and may ultimately take the form of major treks through the mountains.

It is particularly difficult to choose from the abundance of typical examples in the middle and upper school. One which stands out is a project carried out by the Nürnberg Rudolf Steiner School (Germany), in which groups of pupils planted bushes and hedges an a grand scale (15,000 plants in all) in areas where the soil had been exhausted by intensive cultivation methods, and then observed over the years how the plants and animals returned. This — the largest school project ever carried out in Germany — stirred up a lot of public interest and was granted an award.

Then there was the park close by the Waldorf School in Essen (Germany). It had been neglected and had been used by local residents as a rubbish dump. Within the framework of the school's gardening lessons it was cleaned and restored, with the voluntary assistance of the local residents. 'Forest Practicals' of the Rudolf Steiner School of Zürich (Switzerland) take place every year among mountain communities, whose belts of protective forest (these on the steep slopes above the cultivated land) are dying, thus increasing the likelihood of avalanches. The pupils, who fell the sick or dead trees and plant new ones, are very welcome guests in the mountain villages. During a combined land surveying and ecology practical a class eleven of the Rudolf Steiner School in Dortmund (Germany) surveyed a nature reserve in the uplands of Tatra (Poland). The institutions responsible for the area were thus provided with essential cartographical data. Besides these larger enterprises a wide variety of smaller-scale activities takes place; for instance, looking into the issues surrounding waste disposal and avoidance, monitoring a local nature reserve; etc. A yardstick for the success of these little initiatives is the degree of motivation they awaken in the pupils. In every Waldorf school there are groups, both small and large, composed of children of all ages, that devote some of their free time to environmental projects.

Finally it may be mentioned that in class twelve, the uppermost class, every pupil chooses a project and works on it over the whole year. Besides artistic and cultural-scientific themes there are always some on ecology or environmental technology, running from the full investigation of an ecosystem to experiments in solar energy.

The question as to whether there should be a special subject called "Environmental Studies" may be said more or less to have answered itself. Themes related to the environment should run through all subject areas and be dealt with as the opportunity arises. To function properly this depends on the teacher's initiative and commitment, for it cannot be institutionalised. That is precisely what needs to be avoided. It dare not be made into an "obligatory" subject that can be run off routinely without any inner involvement (*cf.* Langeheine and Lehmann 1986). The ecological crisis is by far the most important issue of our time. The survival of humanity is at stake, and the survival of the biosphere. Solutions and remedies can only come from free action undertaken by all.

Summary

1. The attitude of society to environmental protection is ambivalent —- habituation, indifference, suppression are all prevalent. An environmentally conscious minority, among which are many young people, is nevertheless trying to address the problems. School experience shows that in most children and young people there is a latent or open readiness to become environmentally active. This depends upon the pupils being approached in the right manner and being given the chance to identify emotionally with the matter on hand and to be involved in concrete action.

2. The anthropocentric approach to environmental protection is not enough; it must be enlarged by the ecocentric approach, which appeals to idealism. Pure utilitarian thinking has little emotional appeal.

3. An extension of the social conscience beyond human society towards nature is very clearly observable, though still in its beginnings. The highest task of education must be to deepen and strengthen these beginnings.

4. Introducing children to nature must be done in a way in tune with their age. Children in the early primary classes (age 6½ – 9) do not yet objectify the world. Everything around them is animate like themselves, their relation to the environment is still empathic (this condition is not altered by over-exposure to the media; it can, as experience shows, be masked in this way, but not blotted out). All teaching at this level must try to increase friendly attachment and love towards animals and plants. During the transition to a more scientific relation to nature this emotional attachment remains as an underlying support, in time forming the basis of ethical attitudes.

5. In the middle and upper school effort is directed towards understanding complex relationships, as a basis for practical action. Here ecological themes play a decisive role. They must also lead to a richer understanding of the relationship between man and nature, than is generally the case today. Man is not only a "disturbance", but is also capable of working in partnership with nature. This can be substantiated with available factual material, but it must also become direct personal experience, through active caring involvement with nature. From kindergarten in, the whole period of schooling, via gardening and field practicals in farming and forestry, this caring activity forms a firmly integrated part of Waldorf teaching world-wide. This is enhanced by activities in conservation, by nature observation on many different fronts both inside and outside school.

6. Environmental education, understandably enough, has its main point of emphasis in the areas of nature study and natural science. It cannot, however, be restricted to these subject areas, and must run through other

teaching realms as well, according as opportunities arise. The increasing threat to life on earth — an expression of our deeply disturbed relationship to nature — does not permit us to restrict environmental education to a mere subject area.

11

CRAFT AND THE REAL WORLD

Greg Pastoll, PhD

The saving grace of technology is that it is continually eclipsing itself. Just as the stone age gave way to the bronze, then to iron, so will every way of working yield in its turn. Right now the rumble of factories is diminishing before the mesmerising ffft ... ffft ... of the laser printer. But the days of the age of information are numbered even as they begin. On the horizon is a technology which is titivating the human race with the promise of total sensory deception through "virtual reality".

With all this progress piling up in store for us, is it safe (or even sane) to take seriously the topic of hand-crafts? What need can we ultra-moderns have of craft except to assuage our sense of nostalgia? Has craft got anything to do with the real world?

It most certainly has, if the real world has anything to do with the real nature of human beings. The world that our "civilisation" has brought about seems largely to ignore some of the fundamental needs of people. Most types of work fall short on physical exercise, manual dexterity, or creativity. Many types of work consist of manipulating abstractions, rather than engaging with the real world. Our attitudes carry over from our working arrangements, and we begin to relate to others as abstractions instead of to the real people whom the abstractions have come to represent.

The social alienation within our culture became so obvious that not even Karl Marx could overlook it. Yet the root causes of alienation have been mistakenly attributed to a political dispensation, which is itself a species of abstraction. I say mistakenly because Communism's collapse has attested to the incapability of a political system to remedy the alienation. For alienation there are causes closer to home. One of these causes, I believe, is the relative lack of craft-work in most people's lives. I would go so far as to suggest that social health in general would be greatly boosted if craft-work came to be reinstated as a genuinely integral part of our lives.

What do I mean by craft-work, and what distinguishes it from other types of activity? The first point that must be emphasised is that craft in the sense I am using the term has very little to do with the production of trinkets for the tourist market. In connection with such artifacts we can hardly improve on the opinion of Socrates, who once remarked to his companion on a stroll through the Athenian market-place that he was continually amazed at the large number of things he did not seem to need. I would not like craft to be associated with the mere production of curiosities.

I prefer to think of craft as a means to exercising creativity by the "mind-and-hands". The mind-and-hands can be viewed as a single entity, because, in a sense it behaves like one. Who has not regained his equilibrium after a frustrating day at the office by digging in the garden or chopping firewood? The active hand restores the mind.

The converse has been confirmed heartily by psychological experiments in which volunteers underwent sensory deprivation to see what would happen. After several hours of floating idly in a special tank under conditions of minimum sensory stimulation (such as having one's hands held motionless and feelingless in padded tubes), volunteer subjects begin to hallucinate and have to fight down encroaching depression and morbidity. Comfort evidently does not consist in doing as little as possible. We have to be active.

Yet, activity for the sake of it is not enough. It may do wonders for one's physical mood to chop away at a huge log for hours on end. The person doing this, however, would be unlikely to be convinced that his mind was operating at full stretch. Not in the same way, for instance, that would happen while attempting to cast a bronze sculpture or weave an ambitious wall-rug. Craft, therefore, can be distinguished from other healthy active pursuits by the requirement that it provides sufficient creative opportunity to engage the mind (as well as the hands) to the point of enjoyment.

Since creative mental stimulation is an essential feature of craft, it follows that the merit of doing craft-work resides in the *process* more than the product. It is not that the products are unimportant. But if they were produced for the sake alone of using them, then their existence would become more important than the process by means of which they are created. If use alone was the criterion for the worth of an object, then we would be justified in letting machines stamp out every item we needed, and all crafts would disappear. People's relation to material objects, however, cannot be simply one of "use". A factory-made nylon carpet will serve as well as a hand-hooked woollen rug, if insulating the floor is the sole "use" in mind. But a hand-hooked rug has other "uses" which reside in its making, not in its existence.

We must be clear about one of the limitations of craft: to sit before a loom evening after evening is hardly the most efficient means to insulate the floor. But then, to purchase a factory-made rug is no means at all to the exercise of creativity and the furthering of a sense of self-sufficiency.

Self-sufficiency, the stability that comes from knowing that you can do things for yourself, is a vital ingredient of mental health. Regrettably, it is in short supply these days. Dependency on others has become a malaise of our time. Due to the widespread specialisation of work functions, there are often occasions when we are compelled to stand by helplessly while others do for us the things we cannot do.

The plumber fixes the geyser, the city council men remove the fallen tree, the musicians are hired for the party, the garage man obtains the spare part from the suppliers. We may find ourselves limited to watching them at it, while stifling our frustration at what we feel is other people's inefficiency, and on top of that, having to pay for it. (I surmise there is a powerful connection between such enforced passivity and inflation.) Regrettably, a tacit public conspiracy does not permit us to question the right of people to super-specialise in the provision of goods and services. If a demand exists for it, any specialisation is condoned. "That's progress" we are told. "You can't turn back the clock."

One of the arguments frequently called upon to defend a sign of "progress" is the one that it will "save time". In the name of time-saving we have been saddled with endless collections of electrical appliances that are supposed to preserve us from drudgery. In their particular functions these appliances excel, but we are inclined to overlook how much work we have to do to earn enough money to possess them. As for the promise of time on our hands, I would love somebody to explain to me why most people these days are chasing their tails in a mad rush to earn enough money to survive.

If we were lucky enough to have more time at our disposal, what would we do with it? Again, "progress" comes to our dubious rescue in the form of wonderful ways which specialists have invented for us to spend our carefree hours. Most of these ways involve the consumption of goods or services, for example:

- beer, ice cream
- visits to special exhibits (such as Disneyland)
- tours to foreign countries
- TV programmes
- working out at a gym
- riding vehicles for enjoyment.

In each of these pursuits there is a large measure of passivity, which is related not so much to the lack of physical activity as it is to the lack of possibility for originality to be exercised by the person undergoing the "leisure".

In some of the above "leisure" activities, one may detect a certain amount of scope for originality. This scope, however, is often eclipsed by a huge dependence on the infrastructure provided by others. For example, we may feel that the availability of a motor-car extends our capacity for variety and creativity. But we should not overlook the facts that the car was probably designed by someone else, built in some factory over whose processes we have had no say, uses fuel which can only be obtained from limited sources (on their terms), and needs roads, which some agency other than ourselves has had to provide. All these are factors which contribute subtly to the erosion of our sense of self-sufficiency.

It is a sobering thought that all of the leisure activities listed here are nothing more than forms of limited-option consumption. So much for progress! In this type of consumption we are lured by the promise of enjoyment. Participating in these activities is hailed as an experience of progress. The real progress, however, occurs in the direction of diminishing our possibilities for initiating what we feel is worth doing. Progress is also made, in almost every case of limited-option consumption, in the direction of more waste, more inefficiency, more helplessness, and more pollution. These latter trends are beginning to be recognised as undesirable, but we cannot hope to put a brake on them unless we revise our notion of progress itself. It is our misconception of progress, quite as much as the deleterious outcomes of pursuing it, which is rendering the human world alien to humans.

Two vital escape-routes must be opened: we need to begin to live our lives in such a way that we become less dependent on others, and we need to find more opportunities to be creative. The nature of work itself therefore has to be re-thought so that it incorporates more of the elements of craft. I anticipate that this statement will frequently be met by disbelief, and two objections in particular. The first is that craft is an "anachronism", and the second is that craft is somehow connected with the plying of "trades". Firstly, is craft-work truly anachronistic? The term anachronistic is used to describe processes that are no longer appropriate in the context of other developments in human activity. For instance, to be using a horse and cart when everybody else is driving trucks may seem anachronistic. The real test of an anachronism, however, is whether the process is out of touch with the evolved nature of the human being. I do not detect anything about the human being which has "grown beyond" the use of a horse and cart. Some of us may possibly lack the relevant patience, but none of us can claim to have evolved to the point where to drive a cart is alien to our very natures. If the world's petrol ran out, we would all probably revert to horses and carts.

Real anachronisms are more likely to be found in the realm of consciousness than in physical practices. Having acquired a certain level of consciousness we find it difficult to behave at a lower level of consciousness. The thought of carrying on a vendetta, or inflicting corporal punishment or paying a bride-price for example, is reprehensible to some. For such people, these practices are anachronistic.

We should be wary of regarding any practices as anachronistic simply because the age in which they are occurring has been given a fancy label which implies an "advance" in technology. When an age is given a label, it does not mean that every single person in the age in question is actively preoccupied with the prevailing technology. It means only that the user of the label has noticed a pattern of activity, which he or she associates with the age in general. But there are always many such patterns running simultaneously. Right now, on an unprecedented scale, very many people are engaged in the search for meaningful answers to the questions of existence. With equal justification we might therefore easily have chosen another partially accurate label, and have called the present age a "spiritual" one. Hence, the choice of a popularised label for an age is no criterion for the out-of-dateness of any human pursuit, including craft.

The second objection to craft-work is its association with the carrying out of trades, which, by the nature of the servile relationships they engender, are felt to limit the social opportunities of those who engage in them.

A rationale which is sometimes advanced for the teaching of craft-work in schools is that it is a preparation for the later learning of a modern trade, such as that of an electrician, welder or kitchen-cabinet manufacturer. I cannot support this rationale. The only way in which the practising of a craft can be regarded as preparation for a trade is that skills acquired in the one sphere can be put to use in the other. The similarity between the required skills, however, should not be allowed to obscure the differences between the states-of-mind which take root when engaging in the two different occupations.

By plying a trade (and thereby accepting a limited range of options open to one's behaviour) one relinquishes a certain amount of opportunity to decide what is worth doing. One must as a consequence pay undue attention to what other people think is worth doing — a fundamental political sacrifice.

There is thus some truth in the view that trades are cultural patterns which effectively restrict some people to the "practical" stations of life, safely out of competition with the managerial sorts.

By contrast, engaging in a craft does not subordinate the crafter to the will of others. The decisions about what is worth doing, what to use and how to do it remain his or her own preserve. The more scope that there is for originality, the more an activity inclines to being a craft rather than a trade. We see therefore that there is a definite purpose in the teaching of crafts, which has nothing to do with preparing a child for a vocation in the trades. It follows that the inclusion of craft-work in a school syllabus is calculated to have the very opposite effect to that of holding people down.

Human beings need not accept the fate of having to shuttle meekly between passive wage-slavery and limited-option consumption. We all need self-initiated and self-sustaining mind-and-hand stimulation. If we are not getting this, it is time to get off the merry-go-round.

I am sure we can all think of someone we know whose positive disposition to life is fed by his or her engagement with a craft. The happiest man I ever met was a self-taught maker of guitars, who had also been a self-taught professional musician, and who had in the past done quite well from at least one patented invention. To be in the presence of this man was like taking a shower of confidence, enthusiasm and sheer aliveness.

No, craft is no anachronism. We need it more than we may have realised. But it is not sufficient to tack a bit of craft-work onto our lives. Other people will only begin to take the value of craft seriously when they see that it can occupy a prominent place in someone's working life. We will have to revise our conception of work so that each of us does as much as possible of what is needed for our own families. In addition, we need to ensure that whatever is to count as work allows scope for individualised creative input.

If our present life-style does not do us justice, then it is up to us to bring about a life-style that *would* do us justice, one that would give freer rein to the mind-and-hands. Let us not write off craft: it just might be the way forward to the real world.

12

HOW TO DEVELOP FREE EDUCATIONAL INSTITUTIONS AS A BASE FOR A FREE AND CREATIVE HUMAN SOCIETY

Dr Rudolf Mees

In our time it is a well accepted fact that a society without proper educational basis will not be able to develop itself so that its citizens become healthy, worthy and useful members of humanity.

Current educational systems tend to indoctrinate us on the basis of three notions which have to do with the nature of the human being.

- The first of these is the idea that the human being is comparable to a machine. Our brains are said to be very complicated and cunning computers, our heart seems to be only a pump and our digestive system transforms calories into energy.
- A second notion explains the human being as a result of influences from the environment in which it has been living. In this model the human being is seen more or less like a plant that adapts itself to its surroundings.
- Finally, we can be considered as the result of a long struggle for life involving the survival of the fittest, an idea that stems from studying the development and life of animals.

Our modern education does not progress beyond this last idea. Only from the standpoint of religion, but certainly not as part of science, are we allowed to consider the human being as a being in its own right and with its own essence.

Naturally, animals have many things in common with plants and the mineral world. But nobody would confuse an animal with a crystal or a rose with an elephant.

But somehow we don't seem to be able to admit or even suppose that the human being is in essence fundamentally different from these three realms of nature. How did this come about? The answer is not too difficult: nature and all beings therein cannot tell us who or what we are, for the simple reason that we human beings do not find ourselves in the realms of nature and its beings. So we are left to find the answer to the questions who we are *within* ourselves! And with some common sense one can find some very obvious qualities which are unique to the human being.

Although, seen on the surface, we have a lot in common, a closer look reveals that each human being has the consciousness to discover that he or she is an individual, an ego or "I". This individuality experiences during its life a biography, which is not solely written or predestined by circumstances or heredity, but which is also written by the individuality itself. We develop ourselves and want to do that out of our own *free* will. Many of the decisions we take may be attributed to circumstances and other "external" influences, but it would be short-sighted not to recognise that in essence we have the ability to take decisions that are essentially our own.

This means that we can make our own society, change it, create . . . and destroy it. Our whole social life, though in certain aspects comparable to observations in the realm of animals has very definite different qualities and potentials.

One of these is thinking, an activity that derives from the individual ego. One could say that animals can be "clever", but they lack one essential possibility: to create things that nature never produced. Our human thinking has one unique quality: it can think about thinking! And insofar as we may think and believe that a God exists we have also the possibility to deny that existence!

The very fact that our present educational systems do not recognise and work with the fact that the human being is a being in its own right has had far-reaching consequences.

In modern society, especially in the sphere of economic life, we have used human work forces as primitive machines or, as primitive complements of machines. The vast majority of workers in our days have to live and work under these reductionist circumstances, which have been created by human beings.

In social life and politics there is a strong belief that if we improve outer circumstances the human being will "improve" too. Most of our social welfare states were built upon this supposition — yet experience has shown that in the end we find ourselves living, or rather, being lived in an empty shell.

Finally, our whole society is based upon a cognitive, intellectual system of selection. Those who reach the top have "made it". All social organisms tend towards hierarchical structures, pyramids, based on millions of people that haven't "made it".

Clearly one can find the consequences of deductions we have made from observation of the different levels of nature reflected in our educational systems.

Very strongly emphasised in these educational systems is the concept of an input-output model. Facts have to be learnt and memorised and memory (plus a bit of insight) can be tested like a computer through multiple choice methods etc. In order to soften this harsh educational model one can improve circumstances: provide education free of charge (not the same thing as providing a "free" education), adding some "cultural" or "soft" topics, psychological support and so on.

But in the end selection is the core of the whole system: University is at the top of the pyramid, all other "outlets" serving those who could not make it to the top.

These three views of the human being that we characterised have in common that they tend towards creating self-supporting and sustaining systems which in their turn have to fit into the biggest system — the state.

Thus the state can become, by its own quality and nature, the authority that circumscribes and pre-destines the development of human beings that created this state. Truly a prisoners' dilemma!

If we recognise the human being as a being in its own right what kind of education would be appropriate?

- First of all an education that allows a free and individual development of each human being, to the full extent of his or her own qualities and potentialities;
- Secondly, an education that recognises and honours social life and promotes a culture of tolerance;
- Thirdly, an education that offers us the insight and reality that in our working life it only makes sense to serve each other.

Thus the three pillars on which education can flourish are:

- freedom in education;
- recognition of each other as individual human beings;
- discovery of the reality that life makes sense if we serve each other.

These pillars stand on the ground of the recognition that every individual is a free being who is therefore also a responsible being, for freedom cannot exist without responsibility!

This can lead to the conclusion that only a truly free education can — not only in the short term, but for the whole biography of the human being — become an immensely "profitable" (in the sense of "fruitful") investment.

One could then discern *four stages of education:*

The *first period*, until the age of approximately six years, would be spent in the kindergarten or preschool, where we really are allowed to be a child, and to have our dreams and fantasy. The qualities we acquire from these sources provide, later on in our life, the basic faith in life that can carry us through numerous changes and difficult periods.

The *second period* is from six to 12 years of age. We now learn step by step to discover the world through our parents and teacher. Through close co-operation between these important companions of our early life we find the basis that later on enables us to recognise our fellow human beings as they are: it is the forming of a social consciousness.

The *third period* is up to the age of 18 years. We discover ourselves as conquerors of our environment, as critical, thinking beings. In this period we may find a basis for our further biography including our motives for life and work. Our teachers and parents can become examples who inspire us.

The *fourth period* brings us through our adult life, which in itself contains many stages of development. The inner qualities developed during the three phases of schooling enable us to acquire the will to engage in lifelong learning. Changes in life and work are then not experienced primarily as threats, but as challenges to be overcome.

In the first two phases education concentrates on the "opening up" of the child like a flower in all its qualities and potentials. These phases require a free space surrounded by warmth and interest. This free space can be guaranteed by our society by granting freedom to, and expecting responsibility from teachers, parents and boards of schools. State supervision has no added value. On the contrary, such supervision will always tend to limit and manipulate through political forces the contents of this freedom. During the third phase the external world enters more fully into the consciousness of the pupil and will also announce its own interest, to do with society and work organisations. During the fourth phase one could say that further education and development is the responsibility of the person who has now become an adult.

This approach to education requires an adequate way of financing it.

During the first and second stage of education the responsibility lies solely in the hands of parents and teachers. A practical method to finance it would be that the state, through a separate "educational tax" would collect sufficient money to issue vouchers, which can be given to parents for their children. Thus every child receives not only the right but also the financial possibility to receive the education the parents want for their child. Each voucher can have a value that the school can cash in. The whole financial system can easily be privatised: the state only functions as a cashier, and an "educational bank" receives the money and distributes the vouchers that the schools can cash with that "bank". Thus the money meant for educational purposes can only be used for that purpose. Each child has a right per year for one voucher and schools will be free and responsible for the use of the money represented by the voucher. Finally, the system is not open-ended, as each year it can be established how many children are entitled to vouchers.

In the third phase a mixed system could be envisaged. Not only the parents, but also society, has an increasing interest in the individuality to be educated.

What kind of profession is to be learnt and when will that person be ready to start working in society? Thus, for this phase of education part of the finances needed to issue these vouchers, could be contributed by all (profit and non-profit) organisations that employ workers.

In the fourth stage one could imagine that the individual, with or without the help of the organisation where he or she works can save money with the "educational bank" to obtain vouchers for further education. This kind of saving could be made attractive by tax-exempts just like savings for pension schemes.

At present there is a great need in economic life to have people who can take decisions, are creative, see changes as challenges and, above all, love their work. A free educational approach based on the recognition of the free human individual can and will be the answer for society's need to have a creative cultural life based on real mutual and social understanding, realising both aims through a life of work to serve one another. This is the kind of society we all long for. It is hidden as a potentiality within each human being, but can be released through enabling individuals to find themselves through a truly free process of development. The starting point, however, is recognition of the human being as an individual. The goal is to educate individuals who will gladly work for a free society.

13

HOW IT BEGAN : THE BIRTH OF WALDORF EDUCATION

Ralph Shepherd

Spring 1918 — the Great War was coming to an end. Germany lay in ruins, physically, socially and economically. The old order had passed, and the once proud German army was losing ground on every front. As summer turned to autumn the collapse began. Soldiers returned home to chaos. No food, no clothes, no work — and for many, no families.

It was into this social disorder that the rising Communist Party sought to bring about the November 8th Revolution in Germany, thereby adding to an already desperate situation. Most large companies had collapsed, with only a few exceptions, one of them the Waldorf Astoria Cigarette Company in Stuttgart.

The Company was launched in Germany in 1905 by a group of businessmen led by Emil Molt, who bought the name and trading rights. The company was originally founded in America by John Jacob Astor, a German immigrant who made a fortune in the early 1800s. Astor had come from the village of Waldorf in Baden. The famous Waldorf Astoria Hotel in New York was developed much later by Astor's successors. Apart from the name, the Waldorf Astoria Cigarette Company had no links with the American firm.

It was Emil Molt who was to lead and carry the Stuttgart company through the war years of 1914-18. Molt was an active social reformer and an astute businessman and was able to motivate his employees through his innovative ideas and caring nature. Years before the 1919 rise of the trade unions, Molt had established a Workers' Forum in his factory in which employees could converse with management about their ideas and experiences, as well as their grievances in the work place.

He introduced adult education and cultural upliftment programmes for employees and launched a cultural newsletter that was distributed to clients and business associates. The newsletter became so popular that it soon reached far beyond the Waldorf Astoria's circle of influence.

Emil Molt was an active supporter of Rudolf Steiner's social ideas and campaigned actively for the Three-fold Commonwealth Movement, which proposed a human-centred approach to political and constitutional reforms. In this revolutionary model the economic life was to be underpinned by the philosophy of co-operation, instead of Malthus' economic philosophy of competition which had become dominant throughout the Western Hemisphere. The socio-cultural life fostered the freedom of the individual, whilst the third aspect of this new dispensation was to develop the concept of equality as the basis for political life. This three-folding of community structures proposed for the new constitution in Germany and Austria, reflected the Three-fold Nature of Man (see the article *Education for A Civilisation on the Brink* in this volume) and strove for the realisation of the three lost ideals of the French Revolution, Liberty, Equality and Fraternity, ideals which outside a three-fold constitution were themselves mutually exclusive of each other.

More than 80 000 copies of Dr Rudolf Steiner's book, *The Threefold Commonwealth*, were sold in Germany alone in 1918/19. Unfortunately the age was not yet ready for such a quantum leap in consciousness, and the Three-fold Commonwealth Movement was unable to find sufficient support to become a significant factor in the restructuring of Germany and Austria.

Emil Molt again turned his attention to the needs of his workers. Through his experience in the Three-fold Commonwealth Movement he perceived that real inner change for the human being was difficult to accomplish for anyone who had grown up in constrained social forms. Molt noticed that his factory workers were the sons and daughters of factory workers before them and this seemed to apply also to other class structures. Children were inevitably moulded into the class or type of the parent, giving them no chance of a different experience in life.

Molt then asked Rudolf Steiner whether it was possible to create an education for children that could overcome the restrictions of social or class inheritance, whilst retaining the human values of the good, the beautiful and the true. In other words, was it possible to create an education leading to the freedom of the individual? Rudolf Steiner responded positively to Molt's question, for many teachers had in past years approached Steiner for suggestions on how to enliven education, which they felt lacked both vitality and relevance. Many teachers recognised the harmful effect of a purely intellectual education so aptly described by Charles Dickens in *Hard Times*. Rudolf Steiner had spoken of the necessity of addressing education as a basis for social healing long before the outbreak of the Great War. Now the opportunity had arrived through Molt's question.

It should be mentioned here that it was characteristic of Rudolf Steiner that he never initiated reforms himself, but only responded to questions put to him. In this instance he called together teachers and members of other professions interested in education for the first course in teacher training. He gave three courses which have since been collected as the lecture cycles: "The Study of Man", "Discussions with Teachers", and "Practical Advice to Teachers". The courses ran from August 21st to the 9th September 1919. Rudolf Steiner broke new ground in his choice of teachers for the new "Free Waldorf School". He chose people of real stature and life experience who were open to new ideas and had a general love for children, but did not require that they had formal teaching qualifications. More than 1 000 people came to the festive opening of the Free Waldorf School on September 7th 1919 in a large auditorium in the municipal park in Stuttgart. Rudolf Steiner gave the inaugural address, in which he spoke about the goal of this new concept of education as incorporating an enlivened science, an enlivened religion (spiritual life) and an enlivened art.

While Rudolf Steiner was to select and train the teachers, it was Emil Molt's task to find the funds and premises for the new school. It had been agreed by the Board of Directors that the Waldorf Astoria Company would carry the bulk of the expenses, but capital should be found elsewhere. In economically bankrupt Germany this was almost impossible, and Emil Molt was to donate money from his own resources to purchase the dilapidated restaurant known as the Uhlandshohe on the eastern hill above Stuttgart. On Monday 15th September, 250 children of Waldorf factory workers entered the refurbished building and the new movement for educational renewal began.

During the following four years Rudolf Steiner schools were founded in Austria, Switzerland, Holland and England, yet all retained the name Waldorf. In each case the beginnings were quite unique. For instance, the school in The Hague in Holland, which has for many years had more than 1 000 pupils, began with four young teachers who were also parents, and who decided to start a Waldorf school for their children. Led by Jan van Wettum the four young people had attended many of Steiner's lectures, supplemented by their own study and great enthusiasm. Van Wettum was an engineer who changed his profession to become a Waldorf teacher. He and his wife Katrina visited South Africa often in the 1960s and 1970s, and assisted in the development of the school movement in this country.

The Second World War, predicted by Rudolf Steiner as the inevitable outcome of the unjust Treaty of Versailles, in which the sole blame for the First World War was laid on Germany, followed in due course. Another thinker who foresaw the effects of the Treaty on Germany was South Africa's Prime Minister, Jan Smuts. The Nazi government closed the German, Dutch, Austrian and Scandinavian Waldorf schools. The schools in Switzerland, the United States and England were able to continue through the war years from 1939 to 1945.

Following the pattern established by the first school in Stuttgart, all were founded and supported by parents and interested individuals. Having obtained the services of a teacher or teachers experienced in Waldorf education, and raised the necessary funds, these people created the foundation upon which all the new Waldorf schools were initially built.

The two problem areas in founding the schools were the supply of trained Waldorf teachers and finance. In time, teacher training colleges were established in America and in all major European countries. However, financing the schools has always demanded great effort and sacrifices by both parents and teachers.

Today, the proven success of Waldorf schooling has led to many regions in

Germany financing teachers' salaries and in some instances providing capital for buildings from State funding. This also applies in both Holland and Australia. In most Scandinavian countries Waldorf schools are financed by the State. Unfortunately this is not the case in England or in the United States, where Waldorf schools struggle to survive economically. In New Zealand, a change in government in 1988 led to large State subsidies to Waldorf schools being withdrawn for political, not academic reasons. A recent change in government has seen the reintroduction of state subsidies for the New Zealand Waldorf schools.

In the 1960s the Waldorf movement expanded both in the Third World, via Latin America and India, and in industrial nations like Japan. The growth in Australia is significant — there are now 35 schools, giving Australia the largest concentration of Waldorf schools per capita in the English-speaking world. The conservative nature of the English does not lend itself easily to new ideas, and for many years the number of Waldorf schools remained at about a dozen. However, in the past decade there has been the same degree of expansion in England previously seen in other countries. In Scandinavia respect for Waldorf education is such that at some Waldorf schools pupils are not required to write Matriculation examinations for university entrance.

In the United States Waldorf teacher training colleges are recognised in several states, and Masters' degrees in Waldorf Education are recognised by the states of New York and New Hampshire. In Milwaukee, a project to share ideas and methods from Waldorf education has led to teachers from State schools in the ghettos attending enrichment programmes arranged by the Waldorf movement. This pilot programme has helped one State school in a severely disadvantaged area to operate along Waldorf lines. All the teachers were taken through an intensive retraining programme. Reports on the project are promising and a plan is being developed to assist other State schools in Milwaukee to follow suit.

With the collapse of Communism in eastern Europe in 1989, a surge of interest developed in those countries and Waldorf schools have been established in Poland, the Czech and Slovak Republics, the former East Germany, Rumania and in Russia itself. In Moscow a Waldorf Teacher Training College has been opened to meet the needs of the new initiatives in Russia.

There is however resistance against this development, principally from academics whose thinking is moulded by the Cartesian mind-set that views children (and human beings in general) as chemical phenomena in a mechanical universe, that require only "filling up" with food for their bodies and information for their minds. Also certain fundamentalist churches regard Waldorf education as anti-Christian (in their terms) and dissuade their followers from sending their children to Waldorf schools.

In England the Waldorf schools were just ignored by the academic establishment. This led John Davy, former science editor of *The Observer*, to write an article on Waldorf Education for *The Times* of London, entitled *The Movement That Everyone Tries to Forget* (reproduced in this Anthology).

At the invitation of UNESCO, preliminary discussions were held in Paris at the beginning of November 1993 between a delegation from the Friends of Rudolf Steiner's Art of Education and high-ranking representatives of UNESCO, including the acting General Secretary, Colin N Power, and the deputy Chairman of the Education Section, Dr H W Rissom. The goal of these conversations was to discuss possible and actual forms of institutional collaboration on an international level. The content of these negotiations embraced three central areas: participation of Waldorf Schools in the world-wide network of UNESCO project schools, the possibility for Waldorf education experts to be taken onto the UNESCO Commission of Experts, and the inclusion of the Friends of Rudolf Steiner's Art of Education in UNESCO as an NGO member (non-governmental organisation).

(See *UNESCO Brief by the International Commission on Education for the 21st Century,* Appendix 2, page 118.)

Developments in Africa

Today there are more than 600 Waldorf schools and over 1000 Waldorf kindergartens world-wide, with more being founded each year. The Waldorf School in Egypt is a large all-Islamic school, while the Jewish state of Israel has two Waldorf schools, which highlights the fact that Waldorf Education is truly non-sectarian and works successfully with cultural diversity. In South Africa the first school was founded in Rondebosch, Cape Town, in 1960. There are now established schools in the Gauteng, kwaZulu/Natal and Western Cape provinces, while newer schools have been situated in African residential areas like Alexandra Township and Soweto in Johannesburg, as well as in areas such as Kenilworth and Constantia in Cape Town, Assegai in kwaZulu/Natal and Bryanston in Johannesburg. There are fledgling pre-schools in Khayelitsha, Guguletu and Stellenbosch near Cape Town, in Venda and in Pietersburg in Gauteng. There are also two farm schools, one near Pretoria and the other at Winterton in kwaZulu/Natal.

In South Africa there are more than 200 Waldorf teachers caring for about 2,500 children of all races and creeds. Teacher training colleges operate in Cape Town and Johannesburg, while some schools conduct their own in-service training programmes. The interest in Waldorf education has grown beyond the confines of the existing schools, and new initiatives and in-service training programmes are being conducted in the Western Cape, Gauteng and kwaZulu/Natal provinces for teachers from State schools and community schools. Teachers in the state schools are now beginning to recognise in Waldorf the spirit of a true Peoples' Education. The African term *ubuntu* comes out of the concept of African humanism and refers to the idea that "a person becomes a person through other people". Many African teachers see this kind of humanness in Waldorf education.

The most recently opened school in Africa is in Nairobi, Kenya. Their teachers having recently attended the South African Federation of Waldorf Schools' annual conference (1992), the school has applied to be a member of the South African Federation, the first member outside our borders. The picture held by many of the new South Africa as the gateway to Africa holds true for Waldorf education as well.

The closing words of Rudolf Steiner at the training course he gave to the teachers of the first Waldorf school sum up the dedication of teachers who are prepared to sacrifice their scarce spare time to undergo a new training to equip them in their contribution for change and for the healing of the social life in South Africa:

"The need is for imagination, a sense for truth, a feeling of responsibility; these are the three forces which are the very nerve of pedagogy. And whoever will receive pedagogy into himself, let him inscribe the following as a motto for his teaching:

"Imbue thyself with the power of imagination,
Have courage for the truth,
Sharpen thy feeling for responsibility of soul."

Epilogue

I am not an educationist. I am not even a teacher, although my medical degree entitles me to the appellation "doctor", which is derived from the Latin verb *docere*, to teach, hence, one who teaches. However, it would be presumptuous of me to comment critically or at any length on the excellent collection of essays in this book which represent one of the most dynamic and relevant contributions to the future direction of education which I have ever seen. I shall therefore confine my comments to my own perceptions on education as seen by an outside observer, an ex-schoolboy, an ex-Waldorf parent, and a current Waldorf grandparent.

Due to the vicissitudes of World War 2, I went to 13 different schools, all in different parts of England, and with widely different basic philosophies. I have therefore gained a certain amount of insight into education from the sharp end which gave to me new meaning to Mark Twain's observation that he had never allowed his schooling to interfere with his education.

Looking back now, I remember one thing very clearly, and that is that I learned most from the teachers who recognised me as an individual and treated me with kindness and patience. I still look back at them with affection and even love, and I strongly believe that if we are ever to achieve success in education, the heart must be engaged as well as the head. Good teachers should not only be thoroughly versed in the subjects which they teach (which should go without saying) but they also need to cultivate their own personal qualities so that they can with grace step down from the lofty perch on which society has placed them and relate to their pupils as warm, concerned human beings with an evident enthusiasm for the subjects which they teach and those who they are teaching. There is an old Jewish proverb which says "My son, more than the calf yearns to suck does the cow yearn to suckle", and it was Sir William Osler, one of the greatest clinical medical teachers of this century who observed that the most that any teacher could hope for was to arouse enthusiasm in his students for the subject taught. If he could manage to do so, then they would educate themselves. The wide success of the film *Dead Poets Society* seems to indicate that this outlook strikes a responsive chord among the general public.

So where are we in education in South Africa? The one thing on which everyone seems to be in agreement is that it is in a state of crisis. In itself, this may be no bad thing, because a sense of crisis may provide the stimulus to do something constructive about the situation, although too much of it may lead to a Trotskyite state of permanent revolution in which the calm, reflective, contemplative atmosphere required for true scholarship may well be conspicuously lacking. Elizabeth Dostal has pointed out in her essay that the crisis in South African education has, in common with many other Third World countries, two main features. The first is the inadequacy of educational facilities coupled with a heavy bias of advantage towards the ruling class — which in South Africa up until now has meant the white race. The second feature is what she calls "school readiness", which has complex ramifications which extend far beyond the acquisition of a set of basic intellectual facts prior to attendance at school. All the sophisticated educational facilities in the world will be of little use to a family struggling with varying degrees of success against unremitting poverty where the main objective is to convert mouths to feed into hands which can work, and I would suggest that only in a society which has attained a certain minimal level of material prosperity will a love of learning for its own sake become a reality.

There are other aspects to the South African educational crisis however which I believe deserve mention. There is currently a tendency in South Africa to swing away from 'Eurocentric' towards 'Afrocentric' cultural values. Although the reasons for this swing may be all too apparent given the country's stormy and violent history, I would suggest with the greatest diffidence that those locked into this tendency should carefully consider whether there is not another sphere to which they might be devoting their attention which I might term 'Anthropocentric' cultural values; in other words, cultural values which transcend mere notions of race and colour and which are common to mankind as a whole. I believe that it is in this realm that Rudolf Steiner (Waldorf) education comes into its own. One of the greatest advances in the history of the civilised world occurred in 14th. century Italy with the Italian Renaissance, which was typified by a rediscovery of the classical values of Greece and Rome, which in turn had been distilled from the values of earlier civilisations. I sincerely believe that one thing which South Africa and other African countries need is a Renaissance of their own, if only to establish the all-too-easily-forgotten principle that there are things of value in life other than the sordid, money-grubbing frenzy which characterises the prevailing philosophy of most of today's world as it has retreated further and further away from true civilised values.

I also believe that the Renaissance did something else which has never become sufficiently widely realised, and which concerns what has been called the eternal feminine in man; what C G Jung termed the 'anima' in man, and the 'animus' in woman. Jungian psychology recognises that there is a feminine aspect of the male psyche — the anima, and a masculine component of the female psyche — the animus. In societies which do not recognise this fact, and which polarise sexual characteristics to an abnormal degree by suppressing the feminine in man and the masculine in woman, enormous psychological energies may be invoked which can have cataclysmic consequences for society as a whole. Part of the reason for the spiritual heights to which the Italian Renaissance attained was the recognition and fostering of the creative, feminine side of their natures by the men of the time. South Africa has been, and still is an aggressively masculine country with its emphasis on competitive sport and male hardihood. Toughness is the great virtue which is instilled in boys from a very early age, and aggression is regarded as a major virtue in its own right instead of a primeval force which needs to be tamed and given direction rather than encouraging its unrestrained exhibition. Women are overtly or covertly despised because they do not in the main possess or exhibit these qualities. A juxtaposition of this unregenerate macho outlook when combined with the raw energies of an unsophisticated and frustrated populace carries with it enormous dangers which should not, and must not be underestimated, and we are already seeing some of its manifestations in what is becoming an increasingly violent society.

A fundamental change in the pattern of what we teach our children has therefore become urgently necessary, but although a great deal has changed in the political arena in South Africa, one thing remains depressingly the same. The people who hold the true levers of power, the faceless *apparatchiks* of the permanent public service are still very much in place, just as they were during the worst of the apartheid years, and although many of them may be dedicated public servants trying to do the best they can under trying circumstances, entrenched and outdated attitudes still hold sway. In the educational sphere, the Inspectorate, the Examining Boards and those responsible for setting school syllabi have not changed, and given their cultural background and political affiliations are highly unlikely to do so. We seem therefore to be faced with two alternatives. The first would be to sweep them out of office altogether — an almost impossible task under anything less than a revolutionary situation which would in any event mean that there would be nobody with the necessary knowledge and skills to replace them. The second alternative would be to take away from them the power to control the content of education by opening up the whole educational field and freeing it from bureaucratic control altogether, and it is with this kind of process in mind that the African Forum for Freedom in Education (A/F/F/E) has been formed. Based on the European Forum for Freedom in Education (E/F/F/E) it exists to provide a rallying point where those who seek freedom in education can work together at a national and international level.

The educational system of a country is one of the primary determinants of its prosperity and stability in the widest sense, and in South Africa, there is now a window of opportunity to establish a totally new approach to education. Anyone connected, even remotely, with the field of education should take careful note of the essays in this book which contains a message out of all proportion to its size. Education and healing are closely connected, and there is much in this country which urgently needs to be healed. The essays in this book are all based on the Rudolf Steiner (Waldorf) approach to education because the authors, including myself, believe that the Steiner approach comes closest to the sort of education which the country now so desperately needs. This is not to say that all the schools in the country should be Steiner (Waldorf) Schools, but as in Switzerland, teachers should be free to use Steiner (Waldorf) educational methods in any school, whether private or state.

My final point concerns the word 'education' itself. It is derived from the Latin verb *educare* which in turn probably derives from the prepositions *e* or *ex* meaning from, and the verb *ducere* meaning to lead. To educate is therefore to bring forth — *not* to pump in.

Dr Nicholas Lee
19 February 1995

Against all adversity, political, ideological and financial, the Waldorf school movement is rapidly gaining acceptance all over the world, not so much by states and formal education which struggles with the immense social, economic and ecological problems that we find ourselves in, but by parents who are prepared to go to enormous lengths to ensure that the Waldorf schools continue to carry the light of a non-ideological, non-sectarian yet multi-cultural schooling that treats children as children. These parents together with teachers, many of whom have had many years concentrated teaching behind them, are the backbone upon which the Waldorf movement is growing.

This book is intended to give only a brief introduction to the educational impulse of Dr Rudolf Steiner. There is no room in this volume to expound upon the concepts behind Waldorf education, neither is there any need for there exists in print some 100 books on Waldorf education in English. Rudolf Steiner's books and lecture courses are available in this list and a catalogue may be obtained from R S Publications, P O Box 4891, Randburg 2125.

Notes on the Contributors

Prof. Adam Small, M.A.(Phil.), B.A.(S.S), D.Litt., O.M.S.G. South African poet, playwright, philosopher and writer. Head of the Department of Social Work, University of the Western Cape.

Martin Fisher, PhD, businessman, academic, educationalist and intervention consultant, and part-time co-worker with The Novalis Ubuntu College for adult education.

Elizabeth Dostal, M.Soc.Sc., is a management and educational consultant in private practice. She was for many years on the staff of the Institute for Future Research of the University of Stellenbosch. Elizabeth is currently completing her PhD in educational methodology.

Stanford Maher, B.A. Dip.Waldorf Ed., senior journalist, director and public relations practitioner at The Novalis Institute, Waldorf School teacher and lecturer on the Novalis Teacher Enrichment Programme.

Peter King, Pr.Eng., B.Sc (Hons), FSAIMM, trained and worked as a mining engineer, a high school teacher in Waldorf schools and then lecturer at Emerson College and Novalis College. Presently chairman of the Board of The Von Hardenberg (Novalis) Foundation.

John Davy received his OBE for his contribution to science. He was for many years the editor of the Science section of the Observer in London and later became the principal of Emerson College in Sussex where he died in 1987.

Joan Almon is a Waldorf kindergarten teacher with twenty years' experience who serves as a consultant and teacher in Waldorf schools and training programmes in North America and Europe.

John Coates B.A., B.Ed., B.Ed Counselling, ex teacher, headmaster and training college of education lecturer. Currently Novalis lecturer and co-worker working with informal settlement teachers.

Andreas Suchantke, renowned biologist and botanist, international lecturer and teacher trainer for colleges of education in North America, Europe, South Africa and Australasia.

Greg Pastoll, PhD, is an educational consultant at the University of Cape Town. He has worked and taught in the field of engineering, and is interested in all aspects of the educational development of human beings. He indulges in a variety of creative hobbies, hence his observations on the place of craft in human development.

Rudolf Mees, PhD (Economics) (Netherlands), banker and educationalist; member of the National Board of Education for the Netherlands. Member of The Novalis Institute Advisory Board.

Ralph Shepherd, director and founder member of The Novalis Institute. Guest lecturer on cultural affairs at universities, colleges and cultural institutions.

Dr Nicholas Lee is a medical doctor in general practice in the Cape, Emeritus Editor of the South African Medical Journal, Director of the Medical Communication Consultancy and Editor of the Anthroposophical Quarterly of Southern Africa.

APPENDICES

The Von Hardenberg Foundation (The Novalis Institute)

The Von Hardenberg Foundation (which operates as The Novalis Institute) was established in Durban, South Africa, in 1982 as a vehicle for contributing to social and cultural change, by a group of people inspired by the Austrian scientist, educationist and spiritual researcher, Dr Rudolf Steiner. The Section 21 Company (Not For Gain) was registered and Novalis became a legal entity in 1984.

The founding group — Yvonne Oates (interior designer), Carol Ross (chartered accountant), Brian Johnson (architect) and Ralph Shepherd (businessman) — sought to offer their various professional talents in the development of innovative and creative processes for the educational, social and cultural problems of the day. This group was supported by many others including Stan Maher, now an active member of The Novalis Institute's management team. The founding group was based firmly upon the Systems or Holistic thinking[1] of Rudolf Steiner. Over the years, Novalis staff have also been inspired by contemporary thinkers such as Fritjof Capra, Maurice Berman, Stephen Covey, Peter Senge, Vaclav Havel and South African Adam Small, all of whom have striven to expose the inadequacies of the Cartesian or western materialistic view of the world.

Members of The Novalis Institute believe that social and cultural transformation from the current model based upon Western materialism to a more human-centred model must be preceded by individual change. Social change either in the individual or the community requires a paradigm shift in consciousness and not merely the adoption of another ideology, dogma or world view — political, religious or philosophical. A total change in the way in which we see the world or in the way in which we think is required. Such transformation can only be experienced and described in retrospect. The process employed to initiate such a change is based upon personal introspection and contemplation in which personal and human values and principles are considered against the destructive effects of Western materialism. All those people mentioned above, in particular Rudolf Steiner, have written extensively about the exercises and processes involved in acquiring this change in consciousness.

Until recent years, such processes were considered to be the 'suspect' domain of (sometimes dubious) Eastern gurus and of New Age enthusiasts, and were not thought to be worthy of serious consideration. However, with the startling discoveries in atomic theory, which have stood a measurement-oriented physics on its head, together with the continuing collapse of the Darwinian theory of evolution for similarly compelling reasons, mankind is increasingly released from the thought prison of the Cartesian mindset in which the universe was seen as an immense machine, and all living things as chance chemical phenomena within a meaningless time/space continuum. In its place is the concept of an Intelligent and ordering universe to which human beings need to relate.

With this background the first Novalis team initiated a series of projects relating to cultural and social issues. However it soon became apparent that education would become the major focus of The Novalis Institute's work. This meant the establishment of a teacher training programme in which educators would be introduced to a more holistic and effective philosophy and practice of education. Such an approach seeks to completely transform teachers' views of their vocation, the teaching being built around the needs of the child, instead of fitting pupils into an education factory system. Only an enlivened and human education can develop capacities and build the initiative and self-reliance which enable pupils to become initiative-takers and job creators, able to shape their own lives effectively and become producers as well as consumers. This would happen through the founding of a new college, for in the words of Albert Einstein, "The significant problems we face cannot be solved at the same level of thinking we were at when we created them" [2]. In a similar vein we cannot expect the social, cultural and economic problems of our time to be solved by thinking coming from the same institutions — universities or research institutes — who themselves have come into being out of the same thinking or paradigm that created these problems in the first place. Experience has shown that most established institutions can only consider "those innovations that might logically evolve out of the current system" [3]; they seem incapable of considering a radical change in the system itself, that is, the possibility of operating under a different paradigm altogether. Hence the need for entirely new institutions that can operate out of new thinking, new paradigms, uncluttered by the past.

Since 1986 the main work of Novalis has developed in the Western Cape Province and kwaZulu/Natal regions in South Africa, the main office being situated in Cape Town, with a full-time staff of 12, supported by many part-time teacher trainers. Offices have also being established in Johannesburg and Durban to facilitate the development of programmes. In addition, Novalis can call upon support from professional consultants in the artistic, architectural and organisational development spheres who share and support the aims and objectives of The Novalis Institute.

In 1994 the Novalis programmes reached over 1400 state school teachers who were introduced to innovative primary and senior primary courses. These programmes were designed to make education more meaningful for teachers and pupils and relevant to social and vocational needs. During the same period seventy school principals attended the Head Teachers Support Programme that enhances democratic processes, attitudinal change and community development programmes within the school and local community.

Plans are currently being formulated for Novalis to respond to a request from the Department of Education in kwaZulu/Natal region, to establish a Waldorf Education based Teachers College in Durban on a joint venture or share-netting collaborative basis in order to develop and offer pre-service and in-service programmes to future teachers.

Over the next 10 years Novalis hopes to establish colleges of Adult Education in the main centres of South Africa offering creative programmes that will contribute to a new culture of learning in this country.

Over the past two decades thousands of new non-Government organisations — NGOs — have come into being with many innovative ideas and ways to work with the social, educational and economic problems of South Africa. The very existence of these NGOs and the fruitful work that has sprung from them is confirmation of the need for new institutions unburdened by traditional or old thinking to deal with today's problems. Novalis is one of these institutions working out of a new cultural/social paradigm.

The Novalis Institute has a membership for which application may be made. The membership elects a Board of Directors (trustees) who in turn have the support of an international Board of Advisors. The Novalis Institute is a signatory to the Treaty of Innovative Teacher Trainers of the European Forum for Freedom in Education. This treaty embraces fifteen European universities and four major teacher training colleges (this includes major universities such as the University of Bielefeld in Germany, and the University of St Petersburg in Russia).

---

1 Also called Goetheanistic thinking after Wolfgang von Goethe, who, together with Frederich von Hardenberg (Novalis) and William Blake, stood in opposition to the materialistic philosophy of Descartes, the science of Newton and the economics of Malthus.

2 *The Seven Habits of Highly Effective People*, p 42, by Stephen Covey. Simon & Schuster 1994.

3 *The Different Drum*, p 8, by M. Scott Peck. Rider, 1990.

Commission internationale sur l'education pour le vingt et unième siè
International Commission on Education for the Twenty-first Centu

BRIEF - EN BREF - BRIEF - EN BREF - BRIEF - EN BRE

January 1994

EDUCATION FOR FREEDOM AND SOCIAL RESPONSIBILITY: THE RUDOLF STEINER SCHOOLS (WALDORF PEDAGOGY)

"In school the question is not of receiving a complete education, but rather of preparing oneself to receive it from life". (R.Steiner)

Steiner Schools try to advocate a new spirit in a rapidly changing world; a purely materialistic conception of the world and of the human being is no longer sufficient to respond to questions posed in our industrial society. The future requires a fundamental change in our way of thinking: the human individual as an independent spiritual entity should be the starting point for all efforts aiming at the renewal of our society. Based on a profound knowledge of human nature, the principles of the pedagogy of Rudolf Steiner (also called Waldorf pedagogy) can be summarized as follows:

- **All human faculties - Intellectual, artistic, moral -** are developed in an equal manner. The curriculum of each school is individually devised, and there is always a balance between theory and practice. Arts and science subjects are given equal importance. At secondary school level, practical courses on agriculture, forestry, surveying, and internships in industrial and social environments are included in the curriculum.

- **Teaching is considered and practised as an art.** The teachers act like artists whose aims are to help the child to discover and love the world surrounding him or her. Their aim is not to cram the child with knowledge, but to awaken at the right moment certain faculties of the soul, of the inner self. In everyday practice the question is not "what is possible?" or "what goes down well?" but rather "what is challenging and what may best stimulate the pupil at the present state of development?" Therefore children stay together in age groups; there is no selection or early specialization and no repetition. The diversity in every class reflects the diversity of humanity as a fundamental basis for social education. This philosophy is in keeping with the 1966 ILO-UNESCO Recommendation on the status of teachers (in particular provision III).

The teachers' roles are to **awaken** the child's **latent faculties** and allow its **profound individuality** to emerge and develop: they thus help the children to find the appropriate relation between their individuality and physical being, their environment and the present-day society into which they are to integrate. It is this relation which will enable them to make the appropriate use of their freedom. Young people are then able to enter into society not as passive spectators, but as conscious sensitive citizens, ready to tackle the challenges of our times by taking an active part in the transformation of our world.

Organisation and management of the school

Steiner Schools are self-governing and have no school head or director, but are run by the teachers, who all have equal rights and decide on all administrative matters (teaching concept, employment of teachers, buildings, finances, etc.). Based on mutual trust and comprehension, the bonds between parents and teachers are cultivated through frequent meetings. Parents also participate in important decisions and take an active part in school life. This sets an example of democracy to the pupils.

Steiner Schools are private schools, financed partially by the state or the local community, as well as by parents who contribute in a spirit of mutual aid, enabling low-income families to enrol their children also.

In 1993 there exist, worldwide, over 600 Rudolf Steiner schools, 1000 kindergartens, and 500 institutions for remedial education and social therapy. Some Steiner schools are members of the international network of UNESCO's Associated Schools Project.

In France, Steiner Schools can be visited at the Fédération des Ecoles Steiner en France, 5, rue Georges Clemenceau, 78400 Chatou, France, telephone no. (33-1) 3952 6917.

Education in critical environments

The originality of this educational approach and its longstanding practical application all over the world have recently proved to be particularly interesting and fruitful in such disadvantaged environments as slums, refugee camps or in conflict situations, conditions where alternative channels of education often prove to be more efficient than official school systems. The following pilot projects are outstanding examples of the success of this alternative method and they might be of great benefit to other situations and countries:

- Soweto and Alexandra (South Africa): schools in various black townships;
- Shati refugee camp (Gaza strip): Kindergarten and remedial education for Palestinian children;
- Zagreb (Croatia): Kindergarten;
- Favela Monte Azul, Sao Paolo (Brazil): schooling and work with marginal groups and street children using the principles of Steiner education;
- Holywood, Belfast (Northern Ireland): Protestant and Catholic children are taught together;
- Pine Ridge Reservation, South Dakota (U.S.A.): school for Sioux Indian children.

FURTHER READING

Carlgren, F. Eduquer vers la liberté, La pédagogie de Rudolf Steiner dans le mouvement international des écoles Waldorf, Les Trois Arches, Paris, 1992.

Craemer, U. Die Favel-Kinder, Sozialarbeit am Rande der Gesellschaft, Stuttgart, 1987.

Edmunds, F. Rudolf Steiner Education, The Waldorf Schools, R. Steiner Press, London, 1992.

Geraets, T. Stars and Rainbows over Alexandra, Heidenheim, 1990.

Kiersch, J. Die Waldorfpädagogik. Eine Einführing in die Pädagogik Rudolf Steiners, Stuttgart, 1992.

Krampen, I. Self--governed Schools. Case studies. E.Fuchs (ed,), Frankfurt, 1992.

Steiner, R. L'art de l'éducation, Méthode et pratique, (conférences), Triades, Paris, 1993.

(Specialized bookstore: PENTAGRAM, 15 rue Racine, 75006 Paris)

Commission Secretariat :

7 place de Fontenoy
75352 Paris 07 SP
France
tel : (33-1) 45 68 11 23
fax : (33-1) 43 06 52 55
E-Mail : EDXXI@FRUNES21.BITNET

Prepared by :

Ms. Sigrid Niedermayer-Tahri
Assistant Programme Specialist
Section for Humanistic, Cultural and
International Education
UNESCO